To Derek
from
Gma + Gpa

The Wit & Wisdom of Abraham Lincoln

Also by James C. Humes

THE WIT & WISDOM OF BENJAMIN FRANKLIN
THE WIT & WISDOM OF WINSTON CHURCHILL
PODIUM HUMOR
MORE PODIUM HUMOR
INSTANT ELOQUENCE
STANDING OVATION
THE SIR WINSTON METHOD
A SPEAKER'S TREASURY OF ANECDOTES
HOW TO MAKE THE BEST PRESENTATION OF YOUR LIFE
ROLES SPEAKERS PLAY
TALK YOUR WAY TO THE TOP
CITIZEN SHAKESPEARE
"MY FELLOW AMERICANS"
THE BEN FRANKLIN FACTOR
HOW TO GET INVITED TO THE WHITE HOUSE
CHURCHILL: SPEAKER OF THE CENTURY
PRIMARY (novel) *(coauthor)*

James C. Humes

The Wit & Wisdom of Abraham Lincoln

❧ A TREASURY OF MORE THAN 650 QUOTATIONS AND ANECDOTES

WITH A FOREWORD BY

Lamar Alexander

HarperCollins*Publishers*

HarperCollins books may be purchased for educational, business, or sales promotional use. For information please write: Special Markets Department, HarperCollins Publishers, Inc., 10 East 53rd Street, New York, NY 10022.

FIRST EDITION

Designed by Barbara DuPree Knowles

Library of Congress Cataloging-in-Publication Data

Lincoln, Abraham, 1809–1865.
    Wit & wisdom of Abraham Lincoln / James C. Humes.
        p.   cm.
    ISBN 0-06-017244-4
    1. Lincoln, Abraham, 1809-1865—Quotations. 2. Quotations, American. I. Humes, James C. II. Title.
E457.99.H88   1996
973.7'092—dc20   95-38431

---

96 97 98 99 00 ❖/HC 10 9 8 7 6 5 4 3 2 1

To my brother Sam,
whose honesty in
matters both public
and private rivals
that of Abe

Contents

Acknowledgments

Any list of acknowledgments must begin with Carl Sandburg, who first told me tales of Lincoln. His multivolume biography remains for me the richest source of Lincoln lore.

I also have to thank my club, the Union League of Philadelphia, which was established in 1862 to support the policies of President Lincoln. The club library houses hundreds of books and papers on Lincoln and the Civil War. Its curator and librarian, Joan Hendrix, has been very tolerant of my eccentricities.

Another library that gave me help was the Civil War Library and Museum in Philadelphia.

Some friends who gave me suggestions are Federal Judge Franklin Van Antwerpen and Wilma Lewis, who runs a great lecture bureau in Sacramento. Other friends who gave me encouragement are Bill Schulz of Reader's Digest and John Le Boutillier.

Since I do not type, I owe much to Nancy Kowalchik who did the main work and Peggy Whalen who did the rest.

A final note of appreciation to those towns in Illinois that reenacted the Lincoln-Douglas Debates in 1994 and to C-Span, which showed them. I did much of my research and reading with those words of 135 years ago resounding in my ears.

Foreword

The legacy of Abraham Lincoln is not just his preservation of the Union. He gave to Americans our purpose as free men and women and to the world the promise of America to those oppressed by tyranny.

Lincoln said in 1861, "I have never had a feeling politically that did not spring from the sentiment embodied in the Declaration of Independence." At Gettysburg, Lincoln took the Declaration of Independence and transformed it from merely a political act of independence to a universal message of equality. By "equality" he did not mean equality of result but equality of opportunity. He defined the color-blind dream of Martin Luther King, Jr. in New Haven in March 1860. "I want every man to have a chance and I believe a black man is entitled to it."

Abraham Lincoln has always been a hero of mine and that is true for many Americans. For both native-born and naturalized Americans, Lincoln personifies the ideals of our democracy. Born poor, Lincoln was probably the greatest of self-made men.

As I campaign for the presidency, I am reminded of two judgments of Lincoln.

When he was elected to Congress in 1845, Lincoln stayed in a rooming house and left his family behind. He believed in the "rotation of congressmen." Accordingly, he did not run for reelection. Today, he would shake his head sadly at the sight of congressmen moving to Washington and planning to stay there for life.

Secondly, Lincoln told friends that his years in state politics were happier and more productive than his brief stay in Congress. Similarly, I found the challenge as Governor of Tennessee more constructive and rewarding than the five years I spent in Washington, D.C., serving two presidents. Lincoln understood better than almost anyone that we do not elect a president of Washington, D.C., but of the entire United States of America!

Although Lincoln believed in a strong role for the states, he was anything but a passive president. Sometimes his leadership in the war makes us forget some of his key domestic accomplishments. The Homestead Act signed by Lincoln in 1863 epitomizes for me what my party should advocate: it offered to the head of a family—black as well as white, male as well as female—a chance to own their own land if they put in the blood and sweat equity of tilling the soil for seven years. This was not a giveaway. The hard work of uprooting trees and breaking the crusted ground lay before each applicant. In addition, no federal bureau was established. It was done through local government.

Lincoln was a practical visionary. He had a disdain for the extremist rhetoric spouted from both the secessionist South and radical North. Though he would never compromise his ideals, he understood the necessity of bargaining to achieve his objectives.

Yet unlike some politicians today, Lincoln refused to pander to the baser elements of public opinion. Rather he would appeal to the "better angels of our nature." That did not mean, however, parading his religious beliefs. Nevertheless, his spiritual faith was steadfast and the Bible was a frequent source of counsel. His Gettysburg Address, for example, was replete with scriptural references.

When a delegation of Methodist clergy visited the White House and told him, "We will prevail because God is on our side," he answered, "The question should always be are we on His side?" The answer manifested his reluctance to clothe his actions in some kind of divine mandate. The burden was on each individual to apply his private beliefs to public issues.

One verse in the Bible that Lincoln alluded to in his last sentence at Gettysburg has always resonated with me. It is from Proverbs: "Where there is no vision, the people perish." For Lincoln, it was the ideal of the Declaration of Independence, the national commitment to the democratic dream of opportunity for all. Everyone who aspires to be president should have such a vision and a plan to fulfill it.

Lamar Alexander

A bronze lank man! His suit of ancient black
  A famous high-top hat and plain-worn shawl
Make him the quaint great figure that men love.
  The prairie lawyer and master of us all.

—VACHEL LINDSAY,
      "Abraham Lincoln Walks at Midnight"

Introduction

The first time that I remember hearing the name of Abraham Lincoln was from a white-haired man whose lap I was sitting on. When later I was shown a picture of Lincoln, I was surprised to find that he did not look like the overnight visitor at our home in Williamsport in the spring of 1938.

Our overnight guest was Carl Sandburg, who might be called the "Bard of Lincoln" for his epic six-volume biography of our most beloved President.

Sandburg had come to our upstate Pennsylvania city on a lecture tour and we had put him up for two nights. What I remember along with his flat white hair was his twinkling eyes.

Sandburg perched me on his lap and told me that Abraham Lincoln wore a beard because a little girl had written him a letter suggesting it.

One other early childhood memory in that same year in July would etch the legend of Lincoln even deeper. It was a family trip to Gettysburg for the 75th Jamboree of the historic battle. In 1938, surviving Confederate veterans were invited to join their former foes. I remember my older brother pointing out to me a ninety-year-old veteran in Blue pushing a wheelchair that seated a Confederate Gray. One souvenir we brought home that I remember poring over in later years was illustrated cards—about the size of bubblegum baseball and World War II cards I would collect a little later. They were pictures of the various Union and Confederate generals as well as one of Lincoln delivering the Gettysburg Address.

Actually, I once met a man who had seen Lincoln! After my freshman year at Williams College in 1954 I hitchhiked across the country. On U.S. Route 40 through Illinois I was picked up in a Pontiac by a slight man in his late fifties who related to me his eerie experience when he was a twelve-year-old boy in Springfield.

His father was a member of the construction crew that was building a Lincoln memorial in 1904. He had sent a note to his son in the seventh grade to take his bike and come down to the construction area.

Lincoln's body was being moved from the old grave site. As in the Kennedy assassination, rumors were rife that the remains of Lincoln had been tampered with—perhaps even stolen. So it was decided to open the casket to have the remains inspected by doctors and other observers.

My ride-giver related to me that the body looked just like pictures of Lincoln except that the skin complexion had turned bronze and that some hair was protruding from the nostrils and ears. "The head of Lincoln," he said, "had fallen back in the coffin."

When I asked him if the scene ever gave him nightmares, he shrugged and said, "Not really." Still, I had a dream a few nights later about seeing Lincoln in a funeral home talking to visitors.

Ever since the first saints suffered death through persecution, we have known that martyrdom spawns cults, but no saint has inspired the worldwide reverence Lincoln receives.

If democracy is a secular religion, Lincoln is a Muhammad or a Moses. Each year the Lincoln Memorial, in Washington, D.C.—not to mention the sites of his birth and residence in Kentucky, Indiana, and Illinois—draws millions of pilgrims.

As a republic the United States has no monarch—such as Britain—to embody its nationhood. Our icons are paper, not persons: the Declaration of Independence and the Constitution. But if there is a personification of democracy, it is Abraham Lincoln. Lincoln is a Statue of Liberty in the flesh. From the humblest of backgrounds, Lincoln rose not only to head the first democracy, but to spread its gospel and die while defending it.

America is the only nation founded not by a race, religion, or royal dynasty, but by an idea. To those who say that the belief that anyone—regardless of creed, color, or economic class—can find fulfillment is just a dream, the answer is, they are right. It is the American dream. And the story of Lincoln gives substance to that dream.

The Wit & Wisdom of Abraham Lincoln

Abe's Adages

As a former speechwriter for Presidents of the United States as well as for many governors and senators, I can safely say that no one's words are more cited than those of Abraham Lincoln.

Every politician seeks to clothe himself or herself in the language of our most revered President.

The common man, at least in our ideals, is the sovereign of our democracy, and political candidates seek to win the favor of that ruler. Lincoln, in his words as well as his life, is the voice of democracy. His sayings are the secular scripture of those who aspire to be the priests of our civic religion.

Yet, with a few exceptions, you do not find in Lincoln's writings or speeches the fevered rhetoric of the revolutionary such as a Thomas Paine or a William Lloyd Garrison. Lincoln was a career politician—careful in his choice of words, conservative in his general outlook, and contemptuous of populist demagoguery and absolutist extremes.

For most of his political life Lincoln was a Whig, the right-of-center party of his day. Even when he became a Republican he was no abolitionist, even though he accepted abolitionists' support.

Though morally repelled by slavery, he did not insist or advocate the extirpation of slavery in the South but rather opposed the extension of slavery to the Territories.

As communism eventually eroded in this century by the evil of its inherent lie, so did Lincoln think that slavery would die on its own. To carry the analogy further, Lincoln, like our more recent past Presidents, would have opposed the extension of communism but would have distanced himself from those who advocated the direct involvement of the U.S. government to foment rebellion inside the Iron Curtain.

Yet Lincoln did see the American democracy as the "ultimate hope" of a world oppressed by the chains of tyranny in despotic governments. Lincoln read the Declaration of Independence literally. It was not just a document of deliverance from colonial rule, but a truth proclaiming man's natural rights. For that reason Thomas Jefferson was his favorite Founding Father.

Lincoln, however, would never have blurted out like Jefferson that "a revolution is needed every few years to kill off the aristocrats—they are the manure of the revolution." Lincoln would also have abhorred the elitism expressed in Alexander Hamilton's opinion that "the public is a mob."

The "beau ideal" in Lincoln's formative years was Henry Clay, who, like Lincoln, was a fellow Whig and native Kentuckian. Clay was the original middle-of-the-roader—whose loyalty to the Union was the force guiding him to craft two legislative compromises, in 1828 and in 1850.

Clay, not Daniel Webster, was Lincoln's Whig hero. The speeches of the New Englander Webster may have been too grandiloquent for

Lincoln's ears. The border-state Clay was also an orator but less apocalyptic in tone.

Lincoln was a man without prejudice in a day when discrimination against race, religion, and foreign birth was widespread. Yet Lincoln did harbor a distaste for the airs of the pompous and the cant of the pretentious.

A man of humble background himself, Lincoln identified with the aspirations of the working man. America, to Lincoln, was the land of opportunity. His belief in the dignity of man made him contemptuous of proto-Marxian populists who to him were actually patronizing the poor by pandering to them.

ADMINISTRATION
☞ I must run the machine as I find it.

AGRICULTURE
☞ Population must increase rapidly—more rapidly than in former times—and ere long, the most valuable of all arts will be the art of deriving a comfortable subsistence from the tilling of soil.

ALCOHOL
☞ Whether or not the world would be vastly benefitted by a total banishment of all intoxicating drunks seems not now an open question. Three-fourths of mankind confers the affirmative with their tongues and I believe all the rest acknowledge it in their hearts.

AMBITION

☞ Every man is said to have his peculiar ambition. Whether it be true or not, I can say, for one, that I have no other so great as that of being truly esteemed by my fellow man, by rendering myself worthy of their esteem.

☞ I have never professed an indifference to the honors of official station.

AMERICA

☞ All the armies of Europe, Asia, and Africa combined with all the treasure of the earth in their military chest, with a Bonaparte for a commander, could not by force take a drink from the Ohio [River], or make a track in the Blue Ridge [Mountains] in a trial of a thousand years.

☞ Nowhere in the world is [there] presented a government of so much liberty and equality.

☞ We are now a mighty nation; we are about thirty millions of people; and we own and inhabit about 1/15th of the dry land of the whole earth.

☞ We shall prove in a few years that we are indeed the treasury of the world.

☞ There is no such thing as a free man being fatally fixed for life in the condition of a hired laborer.

ANCESTRY

☞ I don't know why my grandfather was; I am more concerned to know what his grandson will be.

APOLOGY

☞ I dislike to appear as an apologist for an act of my own I know was right.

APPEASEMENT

☞ Fearlessness for the right is a better thing than fearfulness for peace.

APPLAUSE

☞ The highest compliment you can pay me during the brief half-hour as I conclude is by observing a strict silence; I'd rather be heard rather than be applauded.[*]

ARGUMENT

☞ Shades of opinion may be sincerely entertained by honest and truthful men.

ATTEMPT

☞ I say "try"—if we never try, we shall never succeed.

BIGOTRY

☞ When the Know-Nothings get control, it [the Declaration] will read "All men are created equal—except Negroes, foreigners, and Catholics." When it comes to this, I should prefer emigrating to some country where they make no pretense of loving liberty—to Russia, for instance—where despotism can be taken pure without the alloy of hypocrisy.

---

[*]Said in the Lincoln-Douglas debates.

BIBLE

☞ This great book . . . is the best gift God has given man. . . . But for it we could not know right from wrong.

☞ Take all of this book upon reason that you can, and the balance on faith, and you will live and die a happier man.

BLACKS

☞ All I ask for the Negro is that if you do not like him, let him alone. If God gave him but little let him that little enjoy.

☞ I barely suggest for your private consideration whether some of the colored people may not be let in [as citizens]—as for instance, those who have fought gallantly in our [military] ranks.

BOOKS

☞ Books serve to show a man that those original thoughts of his aren't very new after all.

☞ I have never read an entire novel in my life. I once commenced *Ivanhoe* but never finished it.

BORROWING

☞ Two things I will not lend; my wife and my carriage.

CAMPAIGN ATTACKS

☞ Every foul bird comes abroad and every dirty reptile rises up.

CAPITALISM

☞ I don't believe in a law to prevent a man from getting rich; it would do more harm than good.

☞ Property is desirable, and is a positive good in the world. Let not him who is houseless pull down the house of another, but let him work diligently and build one for himself, thus by example assuring that his own shall be safe from violence when built.

CHALLENGE

☞ The fiery ordeal through which we pass, will light us down, in honor or dishonor, to the latest generation.

☞ The occasion is piled high with difficulty.

☞ Are you not over cautious when you assume that you cannot do what the enemy is constantly doing?

CHANGE

☞ It is best not to swap horses while crossing the stream.*

☞ The dogmas of the quiet past are inadequate to the stormy present . . . as our case is new, so we must think anew and act anew.

CHARACTER

☞ Character is like a tree and reputation like its shadow. The shadow is what we think of it—the real thing is the tree.

CHILDREN

☞ Love is the chain whereby to bind a child to his parents.

CHURCH

☞ Bless all the churches and blest be God who in this our great trial giveth us the churches.

---

*This colloquial wisdom—more than any discourse on presidential experience—swayed the minds of voters in the election of 1864.

CITIZENSHIP

☞ I appeal to you to constantly bear in mind that with you, not with politicians, not with Presidents, not with office-seekers is the question, "Shall the Union and shall the liberties of this Country be preserved to the latest generation?"

CIVIL LIBERTIES

☞ If by mere force of numbers a majority should deprive a minority of any clearly written constitutional right, it might, in a moral point of view, justify revolution—certainly it would if such a right were a vital one.

CIVIL WAR

☞ Does not it seem strange that I who could not ever so much as cut off a head of a chicken should have been elected or selected in midst of this blood?

☞ The war is eating my life out. I have a strong impression I shall not live to see the end.

☞ This war might have been finished at Antietam if everybody had been in his place who was able to be there—173,000 whom the government was paying—yet [there were] 83,000 absent for action—some in furloughs, [and] leaves.

CLASS SYSTEM

☞ There is no permanent class of hired laborers amongst us [Americans]. I was a hired laborer.

COMMANDER-IN-CHIEF

☞ I think the Constitution invests its Commander-in-Chief with the law of war in time of war.

COMMITMENT

☞ Come what will. I will keep faith with friend and foe.

COMPASSION

☞ I am charged with making too many mistakes on the side of mercy.

COMPLETION

☞ Oh no, I want to see it [the war] out. It's best when you undertake a job to finish it.*

COMPROMISE

☞ The true rule in determining to embrace or reject anything is not whether it have any evil in it but whether it has more evil than good. There are few things wholly evil and wholly good. About everything is an inseparable compound of the two.

CONGRESSMAN

☞ Being elected to Congress—though I am very grateful to our friends for having done it—has not pleased me as much as I expected.

CONSCIENCE

☞ I desire so to conduct the affairs of this administration that if at the end, when I come to lay down the reins of power, I have lost

---

*Lincoln was speaking about running for reelection as President.

every friend on earth, I shall at least have one friend left, and that friend shall be down inside of me.

☞ Would you have voted what you felt to be a lie?*

CONSERVATISM

☞ What is conservatism? Is it not adherence to the old and tried against the new and untried?

☞ In all that the people can individually do as well as for themselves, the government ought not to interfere.

☞ What I do say is, that if we would supplant the opinions and policies of our [Founding] Fathers in any case, we should do so upon evidence so conclusive and argument so clear that even their great authority, fairly considered and weighed, cannot stand.

☞ I do not mean to say that this general government is charged with the duty of redressing or preventing all the wrongs in the world—but I do think that it is charged with preventing all wrongs to itself.

CORRUPTION

☞ What kills the skunk is the publicity it gives itself.

---

*Lincoln's answer to law partner William Herndon, who asked how Lincoln could have voted against popular opinion on the Mexican War.

COWARDICE

☞ If Almighty God gives a man a cowardly pair of legs, how can he help their running away with him?

☞ To sin by silence when they should protest makes cowards of men.

CRISIS

☞ I pass my life in preventing the storm from blowing down the tent, and I drive in the pegs as fast as they are pulled up.

CRITICISM

☞ I can bear censure but not insult.

☞ He has the right to criticize who has the heart to help.

DANGER

☞ We won't jump that ditch until we come to it.

DECLARATION OF INDEPENDENCE

☞ I have never had a feeling politically that did not spring from the sentiments embodied in the Declaration of Independence.*

☞ Do not destroy that immortal emblem of humanity—the Declaration of Independence.

---

*Said in Philadelphia on Washington's birthday in preinaugural ceremonies near Independence Hall in 1861.

DEFEAT

☞ Let us, therefore, study the incidents of this as philosophy—to learn wisdom from them as wrongs to be avenged.

☞ Well, the election is over and the main point is we are beaten. Still my view is that the fight must go on. Let no one falter.[*]

DELIBERATION

☞ I shall go just as fast and only as fast as I think I'm right and the people are ready for the step.

☞ My purpose is to be just and fair and yet not to lose time.

DEMOCRACY

☞ No man is good enough to govern another man without that other's consent.

☞ I have done with this mighty argument of self-government. Go, sacred thing! Go in peace!

☞ The ballot is stronger than the bullet.

☞ The country and the nation belong to the people who inhabit it.

☞ As a nation of free men we must live through all time, or die by suicide.

☞ Our popular government has often been called an experiment.

---

[*]Said at the conclusion of the 1856 Presidential election when John Fremont, the Republican candidate, was defeated.

DESPOTISM

☞ When the white man governs himself, that is self-government; but when he governs himself and also governs another man, that is more than self-government—that is despotism.

DESTINY

☞ I claim not to have controlled events, but confess plainly that events have controlled me.

☞ I believe I am a humble instrument in the hand of our Heavenly Father.

DETERMINATION

☞ Hold on with a bulldog grip, and chew and choke as much as possible.[*]

DICTATORS

☞ Only those generals who gain successes can set up dictatorships.

DISCRETION

☞ I am determined to borrow no trouble.

DOER

☞ He who does something at the head of one regiment will eclipse him who does nothing at the head of a hundred [regiments].[†]

---

[*]Telegram to General Ulysses Grant.
[†]A note to a brigadier general.

DOMESTIC RELATIONS

☞ I have learned a great many years ago that in a fight between husband and wife, a third party should never get between the woman's skillet and the man's ax-handle.

DRUNKENNESS

☞ If we take habitual drunkards as a class, their heads and hearts will bear advantageous comparison with those of any other class.

DUTY

☞ Let us have faith that right makes might and in that faith do our duty as we understand it.

☞ I have done my duty and stand clear before my conscience.

EGALITARIANISM

☞ Inequality is certainly never to be embraced for its own sake; but is every good thing to be discarded which may be inseparably connected with some degree of it? If so, we must discard all government.

EGOTISM

☞ A thousand pretenses for not getting along are all nonsense—they deceive nobody but yourself.

☞ When a great man begins to be mentioned for a very great office, his head is very likely to be a little turned.

ELECTIONS

☞ The strife of the election is but human nature applied to the facts of the case.

EMBARRASSMENT

☞ I have found that when one is embarrassed, usually the shortest way to get through with it is to quit talking or thinking about it, and go do something else.

ENDING

☞ A good consummation is within an easy reach—do not let it slip.

ENVIRONMENT

☞ Let us hope by the best cultivation of the physical world beneath and around us, and the intellectual and moral world within us, we shall secure an individual, social, and political prosperity and happiness whose course shall be onward and upward and which, while the earth endures, shall not pass away.

ETHICS

☞ Some things that are legally right are not necessarily morally right.

☞ Some men seem to think that as long as they keep out of jail they have a sure chance of getting into heaven.

EXCUSES

☞ I fear explanations—explanatory of things explained.[*]

EXPERIENCE

☞ We dare not disregard the lessons of experience.

---

[*]Said to Douglas about his rationalization of his slavery position.

☞ I don't think much of a man who is not wiser today than he was yesterday.

EXTREMISM

☞ An enthusiast broods over the oppression of a people till he fancies himself commissioned by Heaven to liberate them.

☞ In grave emergencies, moderation is generally safer than radicalism.

FACTS

☞ I am a firm believer in the people. If given the truth, they can be depended upon to meet any national crisis. The great point is to bring them the real facts.

FAREWELL

☞ I now leave, not knowing when, or whether ever I may return, with a task before me greater than that which rested upon Washington. Without the assistance of that Divine Being, who ever attended man, I cannot succeed. With that assistance I cannot fail.*

FLAG

☞ If I can have the same general cooperation of the people of this nation, I think the flag of our country may be kept flying gloriously.

---

*Spoken on Lincoln's departure from Springfield in February 1861.

FORGIVENESS
☞ I choose always to make my statute of limitations a short one.

FREEDOM
☞ I intend no modification of my oft-expressed wish that all men everywhere could be free.

☞ My faith in the proposition that each man should do precisely as he pleases, which is exclusively his own, is at the foundation of the sense of justice that is in me. I extend the principle to communities of men as well as individuals. I so extend it because it is politically wise, as well as naturally just; politically wise in saving us from broils about matters which do not concern us.

☞ Among free men there can be no successful appeal from the ballot to the bullet.

☞ In giving freedom to the slave, we assure freedom to the free—honorable alike in what we give and what we preserve.

☞ Those who deny freedom to others deserve it not for themselves.

FREE SOCIETY
☞ When one starts poor, as most do in the race of life, free society is such that he knows he can better his condition; he knows there is no fixed condition of labor for his whole life.

☞ Let everyone who really believes, [be] resolved that free society is not and shall not be a failure.

FRIENDS

☞ The loss of enemies does not compensate for the loss of friends.

☞ The better part of one's life consists of friendships.

FUTURE

☞ Let us hope that by the best cultivation of the physical world, beneath and around us, and the intellectual and moral world within us, we shall secure an individual, social, and political prosperity and happiness whose course shall be onward and upward and which, while the earth endures, shall not pass away.

GENIUS

☞ Towering genius disdains a beaten path.

GOD

☞ I've been driven many times to my knees by the overwhelming conviction that I had nowhere else to go.

☞ The Almighty has His own purposes.

☞ The will of God prevails. In great contests each party claims to act in accordance with the will of God. Both *may* be, and one *must* be wrong. God cannot be *for* and *against* the same thing at the same time.

☞ The purposes of the Almighty are perfect and must prevail though we for many months may fail to accurately perceive them in advance.

☞ I have often wished that I was a more devout man than I am. Nevertheless, amid the greatest difficulties of my administration, when I could not see any other resort, I would place my whole reliance in God, knowing that all would go well and that He would decide for the right.

☞ I believe in Him whose will, not ours, is done.

GOVERNMENT
☞ Must a government of necessity be too strong for the liberties of its own people or too weak to maintain its own existence?

☞ From this appears that if all men were just, there still would be need for some, but not much, government.

☞ Government is a combination of the people of a country to effect certain objects by joint effort. The best framed and best administered governments are necessarily expensive—while by errors in frame and maladministration, most of them are more onerous than they need be, and some of them are then very oppressive.

☞ It is safe to assert that no government proper ever had a provision in its organic law for its own termination.

☞ The legitimate object of governments is to do for a community of people, whatever they need to have done, but cannot do *at all* or cannot, *so well* do for themselves—in their separate and individual capacities.

HAPPINESS
☞ Most folks are about as happy as they make up their minds to be.

HEIGHT

☞ In my opinion, a man's legs ought to be long enough to reach the ground.

HISTORY

☞ We cannot escape history.

☞ I don't know much of history and all I do know of it I have learned from law books.

HOMETOWN

☞ I like to see a man proud of the place in which he lives. I like to see a man live in it so that his place will be proud of him.

HONESTY

☞ All that I am in the world—the Presidency and all else—I owe to that opinion of me which the people express when they call me "honest Old Abe."

☞ I have always wanted to deal with everyone I meet candidly and honestly. If I have made any assertion not warranted by facts, and it is pointed out to me, I will withdraw it cheerfully.

HOUSING

☞ In regard to the homestead law, I have to say that in so far as the government lands can be disposed of, I am in favor of cutting up the wild lands into parcels, so that every poor man may have a home.

HUMAN NATURE

☞ Human action can be modified to some extent but human nature cannot be changed.

☞ All mankind in the past, present and future in all action are moved—controlled by a nature—at bottom the sickly tongue of selfishness.

☞ He that knows anything of human nature doubts that interests will prevail over duty.

HUMANITY
☞ I want it said of me that I always plucked a thistle and planted a flower when I thought a flower would grow.

HUMOR
☞ With the fearful strain that is on me night and day, if I did not laugh I should die.

IDEALS
☞ Organizations rallied around principles may, by their own dereliction, go to pieces, but the principle will remain and will reproduce another . . . till the final triumph will come.

IMMIGRATION
☞ I have no doubt of the power and duty of the executive, under the law of nation, to exclude enemies of the human race from asylum in the United States.

IMPROVEMENT
☞ Whether I shall ever be better I cannot tell; I awfully forebode that to remain as I am is impossible; I must die or be better.

INCONSISTENCY
☞ I shall try to correct errors when shown to be errors, and I shall adopt new views so fast as they shall appear to be new views.

INDEPENDENCE HALL
☞ I have never asked anything that does not breathe from those walls. All my political warfare has been in favor of the teaching coming forth from that sacred hall. May my right hand forget its cunning and my tongue cleave to the roof of my mouth if I prove false to those teachings.

INDUSTRY
☞ Work, work, work is the main thing.

INFALLIBILITY
☞ I cannot claim that I am free from error in all the opinions that I advance.

INJUSTICE
☞ The best way to get a bad law repealed is to enforce it strictly.

INTELLECTUALISM
☞ Let us be diverted by none of those sophisticated contrivances wherewith we are so industriously plied and belabored.

INTERFERENCE
☞ If you go to mixing in a mix-up, you only make the muddle worse.

JESUS CHRIST
☞ The fundamental truths reported in the four gospels as from

the lips of Jesus Christ, and that I first heard from the lips of my mother, are settled and fixed moral precepts with me.

JURY

☞ A jury too frequently has at least one member more ready to hang the panel than hang the traitor.

☞ There are two things even God Almighty doesn't know: how a jury will decide, and who a widow will marry.

LABOR

☞ Few can be induced to labor exclusively for posterity.

☞ Labor in this country is independent and proud. Capital is the only fruit of labor, and would never have existed if labor had not first existed. Labor is the superior of capital and deserves much more the higher consideration.

☞ As labor is the common burden of our race, so the effort of some to shift the burden onto the shoulders of others is the great durable curse of the race.

☞ I hold that if the Almighty had ever made a set of men that should do all the eating and none of the work, He would have made them with mouths only and no hands, and if He had ever made another class that He intended should do all the work and no eating, He would have made them with hands only and no mouths.

☞ Thank God, we have a system of labor where there can be a strike.

LAME DUCK

☞ I usually find out that a senator or representative out of business is sort of a *lame duck.**

LANGUAGE

☞ Civilized man is marked off from the savage by the alphabet.

LAUGHTER

☞ Laughter . . . the joyous, beautiful, universal evergreen of life.

LAW AND ORDER

☞ Let every man remember that to violate the law is to trample on the blood of his father.

LAWYERS

☞ As a peacemaker the lawyer has a superior opportunity of being a good man.

☞ There is a vague popular belief that lawyers are necessarily dishonest. I say *vague* because consider to what extent confidence and honors are reposed in and conferred upon lawyers by the public at large.

☞ The leading role for the lawyer is diligence.

☞ Discourage litigation. Persuade your neighbor to compromise whenever you can.

---

*Lincoln was the first to use "lame duck" to define a politician whose elected term is running out.

☞ There are those who are better lawyers than gentlemen.

☞ In law it is good policy never to plead what you need not—lest you oblige yourself to prove what you cannot.

LIBERTY

☞ I am for the people of the whole nation doing just as they please in all matters which concern the whole nation; for that of each part doing just as they choose in all matters which concern no other part; and for each individual doing just as he chooses in *all matters* which concern nobody else.

☞ Many free countries have lost their liberty and ours may lose hers—but if she shall, be it my proudest pleasure not that I was the last to desert but that I never deserted her.

☞ I believe it is the inalienable right of man . . . to be *happy* or *miserable* at his own election and I for one make choice of the former alternative.

☞ I leave you, hoping that the lamp of liberty will burn in your bosoms until there shall no longer be a doubt that all men are created equal.

☞ The world has never had a good definition of the word liberty.*

☞ Our defense is in the preservation of the spirit which prizes liberty as the heritage of all men, in all lands everywhere. Destroy

---

*Lincoln is alluding to the paradox that absolute liberty is anarchy in which one man's freedom could jeopardize another's.

this spirit and you have planted the seeds of despotism around your own doors.

☞ What constitutes the bulwark of our liberty and independence? It is not our crowning battlements, our bustling seacoasts, the guns of our war steamers, or the strength of our gallant army. These are not our reliance against a resumption of tyranny in our land. All of them may be turned against our liberties without making us stronger or weaker for the struggle.

LIES

☞ No man has a good enough memory to make a successful liar.

☞ Deceit and falsehood—especially if you have a bad memory— are the worst enemies a fellow can have.

LOGROLLING

☞ You may burn my body to ashes and scatter them to the winds of heaven, you may drag my soul down to the regions of darkness and despair to be tormented forever but you will never get me to support a measure which I believe to be wrong— although by doing so I may accomplish what I believe to be right.

LOOKS

☞ No one ever expected me to be President. In my poor, lean, lank face nobody has ever seen any cabbages were sprouting.*

---

*In Lincoln's day men of full face and stately figure were considered to have the features of statesmen. He said this in comparison to the round face of Stephen Douglas in his debate with him.

MAGNANIMITY

☞ I have not willingly planted a thorn in any man's bosom.

☞ I shall do nothing through malice; what I deal with is too vast for malice.

MAJORITY

☞ A majority held in restraint by constitutional checks and limitations, and always changing easily with deliberate changes of popular opinion and sentiments, is the only true sovereign of a free people.

☞ If by the mere force of numbers, a majority should deprive a minority of any clearly written constitutional right, it might, in a moral point of view, justify revolution—certainly if such a right were a vital one.

☞ A constitutional majority is the only true sovereign of a free people.

MANDATE

☞ The most reliable indication of public purpose in this country is derived through our popular elections.

MARRIAGE

☞ I have come to the conclusion never again to think of marrying and for this reason: I can never be satisfied with anyone who would be blockheaded enough to have me.

☞ Nothing new here except my marrying, which to me is a matter of profound wonder.

☞ There is no condition (evil as it may be in the eye of reason) which does not include, or seem to include, when it has become familiar, some good, some redeeming or reconciling qualities. I agree, however, that marriage is not one of these.

☞ Marriage is neither heaven nor hell; it is simply purgatory.

MATERIALISM
☞ I believe that—intoxicated with unbroken success—we have become too self-sufficient to feel the necessity of redeeming and preserving grace—too proud to pray to the God that made us.

MEDICINE
☞ It is ill jesting with the joiner's [carpenter's] tools, worse with the doctor's.

MERCY
☞ I have always found that mercy bears richer fruits than strict justice.

MILITARY OCCUPATION
☞ Follow law, and forms of law as far as convenient.

MILITARY STRATEGY
☞ We have greater numbers. Menace the enemy with superior forces at different points at the same time. If he weakens one to strengthen the other—forbear to attack the strengthened one but seize and hold the weakened one.

MISCEGENATION
☞ I protest against the counterfeit logic that because I do not want a woman for a slave, I must necessarily want her for a wife. I need not have her for either. I can just leave her alone.

MISSISSIPPI

☞ The Father of Waters goes unvexed to sea.[*]

MOB

☞ There is no grievance that is a fit object for redress by mob law.

☞ Your hisses will not blow down the walls of justice.

☞ I mean the increasing disregard for law which pervades the country—the growing disposition to substitute the wild and furious passions in lieu of the sober judgements of courts, and the worse than savage mobs for the executive ministers of justice. . . . By the operation of this mobocratic spirit, which all must admit now abroad in the land, the strongest bulwark of any government, and particularly of those constituted like ours, may effectually be broken down and destroyed.

MONEY

☞ The plainest print cannot be read through a gold eagle.[†]

☞ Financial success is purely metallic. The man who gains it has four metallic attributes—gold in his palm, silver on his tongue, brass in his face, and iron in his heart.

MONOPOLIES

☞ These capitalists generally act harmoniously, and in concert, to fleece the people.

---

[*]Said upon the receipt of the surrender of Vicksburg, Mississippi.

[†]Lincoln is referring to the exploitation by military contractors. He liked to dramatize the point by placing a gold coin over a scriptural verse.

MORAL TURPITUDE
☞ A rat gnaws alone and so does a moral weakness within us even though we know it is securely hidden.

MORALITY
☞ I desire to see the time when education, and by its means, morality, sobriety, enterprise, and industry, shall become much more general than at present.

MOTHER
☞ All that I am or hope to be I owe to my angel mother.

NONINVOLVEMENT
☞ The man who stands by and says nothing when the peril of his government is discussed cannot be misunderstood. If not hindered, he is sure to help the enemy; much more if he talks ambiguously—talks for his country with "but's," "ifs," and "ands."

OPPONENTS
☞ Let us all be so quiet that the adversary shall not be notified.

OPPORTUNITY
☞ It is a struggle for maintaining in the world that form and substance of government whose leading object is to elevate the condition of men—to lift artificial weight from all shoulders to clear the paths of laudable pursuit for all—to afford all an unfettered start and a fair chance in the race of life.

OPPOSITION
☞ It is no pleasure to me to triumph over anyone.

☞ I do not impugn the motives of anyone opposed to me.

☞ Did we brave all *them* [crises] to *falter—now*—when that same enemy is wavering—dissevered and belligerent?

☞ I cannot afford to punish every person who has seen fit to oppose my election.

PASSION

☞ We must be led by excitement and passion to do that which our sober judgments would not approve in our cooler moments.

PATIENCE

☞ If we have patience, if we restrain ourselves, if we allow ourselves not to run off in a passion, I still have confidence that the Almighty, the Maker of the Universe, will—through the instrumentality of this great and intelligent people—bring us through this.

☞ Nothing valuable was ever lost by taking time.

PATRIOTISM

☞ Gold's good in its place but living, brave, and patriotic men are better than gold.

☞ True patriotism is more holy than false piety.

PATRONAGE

☞ I have more pegs than holes to put them in.

☞ If ever this free people—if this government itself is ever demoralized, it will come from this incessant human wriggle and struggle for office, which is but a way to live without work.

☞ This struggle and scramble for office, for a way to live without work, will finally test the strength of our institutions.

☞ There are no emoluments that properly belong to patriotism.

PEACE

☞ Peace does not appear as distant as it did. I hope it will come soon and come to stay and so come to be worth the keeping in all future time.

PEOPLE

☞ Why should there not be a patient confidence in the ultimate justice of the people? Is there any better or equal hope in the world?

☞ The people, when they rise to mass in behalf of union and the liberty of their country, truly may it be said: the gates of Hell cannot prevail against them.

☞ Remember, keep close to the people—they are always right and will mislead no one.

PERSUASION

☞ I believe in the providence of the most men—the largest purse, and the longest cannon.

PLANNING

☞ No exclusive and inflexible plan can safely be prescribed as to detail and collaterals. Such exclusive and inflexible plans would surely become a new entanglement.

POLICY

☞ My policy is to have no policy.

POLITICIANS

☞ You may deceive all the people part of the time and part of the people all the time, but not all the people all the time.

☞ The difference between the abstract and specific: you oppose a bill creating more officers . . . then you ask all your friends to be appointed [to those posts].*

POVERTY

☞ No men living are more worthy to be trusted than those who toil up from poverty—none less inclined to take or touch which they have not honestly earned.

PRACTICE

☞ Practice proves more than theory.

PRAGMATISM

☞ I am compelled to take a more practical and unprejudiced view of things.

PREACHER

☞ When I hear a man preach, I like to see him act as if he were fighting bees.

PREMONITION

☞ I shall meet with some terrible end.

PRESIDENCY

☞ I must in all candor say I'm not fit for the presidency.†

---

*Letter written to a Republican senator.

†Said in 1859 when he was first asked if he was considering a race for the presidency.

☞ I happen, temporarily, to occupy this White House. I am a living witness that any one of your children may look to come here as my father's child has.*

☞ I shall do my utmost that whoever is to hold the helm for the next voyage shall start with the best possible chance to save the ship.

☞ It is true that while I hold myself, without mock modesty, the humblest of all individuals that have ever been elevated to the presidency, I have a more difficult task to perform than any one of them.

☞ While the people retain their virtue and vigilance, no administration—by any extreme of wickedness and folly—can very seriously injure the government in the short space of four years.

☞ I take the offered oath today with no mental reservations.†

☞ I have been selected to fill an important office for a brief period, and am now invested with an influence which will soon pass away; but should my administration prove to be a very wicked one, or what is more probably a very foolish one, if you, the people are true to yourselves and the Constitution, there is but little harm I can do, thank God.

☞ Put a man in my place [the presidency] and every weakness will grow a beard.

---

*Lincoln is addressing a regiment of Union soldiers during the Civil War.
†Lincoln's words in his first inaugural address in March 1861.

☞ I may not have made as great a President as some other man, but I believe I have kept these discordant elements together as well as any one could.

☞ Only events can make a President.

☞ The presidency is no bed of roses.

☞ I cannot run this thing on the theory that every office holder must think I am the greatest man in the nation and I will not.

PRINCIPLES
☞ My politics are short and sweet like the old woman's dance.

☞ Important principles may and must be flexible.

☞ The probability that we may fail in the struggle ought not to deter us from the support of a cause we believe to be great.

☞ Stand by your principles, stand by your guns, and victory complete and permanent is sure at last.

☞ Our principle, however baffled or delayed, will finally triumph.

PROBLEMS
☞ Killing the dog does not cure the bite.

☞ The smallest [problems] are often the most difficult things to deal with.

PROCRASTINATION
☞ Leave nothing for tomorrow which can be done today.

PROGRESS
☞ I'm a slow walker but I never walk backwards.

PROMISES
☞ We must not promise what we ought not, lest we be called on to perform what we cannot.

PUBLIC OPINION
☞ There is both a power and magic in public opinion.

☞ A universal feeling, whether founded or ill-founded, cannot be safely disregarded.

☞ No policy that does not rest upon philosophical public opinion can be permanently maintained.

☞ Public opinion in this country is everything.

PUBLIC SPEAKING
☞ Wisdom and patriotism, in a public office, under institutions like ours, are wholly inefficient and worthless, unless they are sustained by the confidence and devotion of the people.

☞ I always assume my audiences are wiser than I am, and I say the most sensible thing I can to them and I never found that they did not understand me.

☞ Don't shoot too high. Aim low and the common people will understand you.

PURPOSE
☞ I think you would do well to express without passion, threat,

or appearance of boasting, but nevertheless with firmness, the purpose of yourself and your state.*

☞ If we could know first where we are and whither we are tending we could better judge what to do and how to do it.

REASON
☞ Reason—cold, calculating, unimpassioned reason—must furnish all the materials for our future support and actions.

REBELLION
☞ Those who fairly carry an election can fairly suppress a rebellion.

REFORM
☞ Our republican robe is soiled and trailed in the dust. Let us . . . wash it white in the spirit, if not the blood of the revolution.

☞ To be able to raise a cause which shall produce an effect.

REFORMER
☞ The pioneer in any movement is not generally the best man to carry that movement to a successful issue. It was so in the old times; Moses began the emancipation of the Jews, but didn't take Israel to the Promised Land after all. He had to make way for Joshua to complete the work.

---

*From a letter to Governor Andrew Curtin at the beginning of the Civil War.

☞ It looks as if the first reformer of a thing has to meet such a hard opposition and get so battered and bespattered, that afterward, when people find they have to accept his reform, they will accept it more easily from another man.

RELIGION

☞ Any man who wants to disrupt this Union needs all the religion in sight to save him.

☞ Probably it is to be my lot to go on in a twilight, feeling and reasoning my way through life, as a questioning [and] doubting Thomas did. But in my poor, maimed, withered way, I bear with me as I go on a seeking spirit of desire for a faith that was with him of the olden time, who, in his need, as I in mine, exclaimed, "Help thou my unbelief."

☞ I do not see that I am more astray—though perhaps in a different direction—than many others whose points of view differ widely from each other in the sectarian denominations. They all claim to be Christians, and interpret their several creeds as infallible ones. I doubt the possibility or propriety of settling the religion of Jesus Christ in the models of man-made creeds and dogmas.

RELIGIOSITY

☞ Men are not flattered by being shown that there has been a difference of purpose between the Almighty and them.

REPENTANCE

☞ It is the duty of nations as well as men to confess their sins and transgressions in humble sorrow yet with assured hope that genuine repentance will lead to mercy and pardon.

REPUBLICAN PARTY

☞ Republicans are for both man and the dollar but in case of conflict the man before the dollar.

RESEARCH

☞ I know of nothing so pleasant to minds as the discovery of anything which is at once *new* and *valuable*; for nothing which so lightens and sweetens toil, as the hopeful pursuit of such discovery.

RESOLUTION

☞ Having chosen our course, without guile and with pure purpose, let us renew our trust in God and go forward without fear and with manly hearts.

☞ I am not bound to win, but I am bound to be true. I am not bound to succeed, but I am bound to live up to what I have. I must stand with anybody that stands right and part company with him when he goes wrong.

☞ Hold firm with a chain of steel.

☞ Still let us not be oversanguine of a speedy triumph. Let us be quite sober. Let us diligently apply the means, never doubting that a just God in his own good time will give us the rightful result.

☞ I think it cannot be shown that once taken a position, I have ever retreated from it.

☞ Keep pegging away!

☞ Remember how long you have been in setting out on the true course; how long you have been in getting your neighbors to understand and believe as you now do. Stand by your principles, stand by your guns, and victory—complete and permanent—will be yours.

RESPONSIBILITY
☞ In times like the present men should utter nothing for which they would not willingly be responsible through time and eternity.

REVOLUTION
☞ Any people anywhere, being inclined and having the power, have the right to rise up and shake off the existing government and form one that suits them better.

☞ Be not deceived. Revolutions do not go backwards.

RIDICULE
☞ I have endured a great deal of ridicule without much malice and have received a great deal of kindness not quite free of ridicule.

SECESSION
☞ No state upon its mere motion can lawfully get out of the Union; resolves and ordinances to that effect are legally void.

SLAVERY
☞ Whenever I hear anyone arguing for slavery, I feel a strong impulse to see it tried on him personally.

☞ In our greedy chase to make profit of the Negro let us beware—lest we cancel and tear to pieces even the white man's chance of freedom.

☞ In giving freedom to the slave we assure freedom to the free—honorable alike in what we give and what we preserve.

☞ Slavery is somewhat like the vein that you see on the back of a man's neck. If it were cut off immediately without the necessary precautions, the man could easily bleed to death. However, if it were allowed to grow unattended, and without any kind of medical surgery, it could easily spread until it would completely disfigure or incapacitate the man. As the man must submit to carefully planned surgery to save his life from being destroyed by the vein, so must the nation carefully and tolerantly treat the problem of slavery in a way so as not to destroy the Union.

☞ As I would not be a *slave* so I would not be a *master.*

☞ It is the eternal struggle between these two principles—right and wrong—throughout the world. They are two principles that have stood face to face from the beginning of time; and will ever continue to struggle. The one is the common right of humanity, and the other the divine right of kings. It is the same principle in whatever shape it develops itself. It is the same spirit that says, "You toil and work and earn bread, and I'll eat it." No matter in what shape it comes, whether from the mouth of a king who seeks to bestride the people of his own nation and live by the fruit of their labor, or from one race of men as an apology for enslaving another race, it is the same tyrannical principle.

☞ When I see strong hands sowing, reaping, and threshing wheat into bread, I cannot refrain from wishing and believing that those hands, some way in God's good time, shall own the mouth they feed.

☞ If we cannot give freedom to every creature, let us do nothing that will impose slavery upon any other creature.

☞ If I ever get a chance to hit this thing, I'll hit hard.*

SMALL TALK
☞ I shall never be old enough to speak without embarrassment when I have nothing to talk about.

SOPHISTRY
☞ A specious and fantastic arrangement by which a man can prove a horse-chestnut to be a chestnut horse.

SORROW
☞ In this sad world of ours, sorrow comes to all and to the young it comes with bittersweet agony, because it takes them unawares.

STATESMANSHIP
☞ Honest statesmanship is the wise employment of individual meannesses for the public good.

SUCCESS
☞ Always bear in mind that your own resolution to succeed is more important than any other thing.

☞ All rising to a great place is by a winding stair.

---

*Reported to have been said to his cousin Dennis Hanks.

SUPPORT

☞ I distrust the wisdom—if not the sincerity of my friends— who would hold my hands while my enemies stab me.

SUPREME COURT

☞ If the policy of the government upon vital questions affecting the whole people is to be irreversibly fixed by the decisions of the Supreme Court . . . the people will have ceased to be their own rulers, having to that extent practically resigned their government into the hands of that eminent tribunal.

SYMPATHY

☞ I need success more than sympathy.

TACT

☞ Tact is the ability to describe others as they see themselves.

TALK

☞ Better to remain silent and thought a fool than to speak out and remove all doubt.

TAXES

☞ I do not like this punishment of withholding pay: it falls so very hard on poor families.

TEMPERANCE

☞ Prohibition will work great injury to the cause of temperance.

THEATER

☞ A farce or a comedy is best played; a tragedy is best read at home.

TIME

☞ *Time! What an empty vapor 'tis*
*And days how swift they are!**

☞ Time is everything. Please act in view of this.

TRUST

☞ If you once forfeit the confidence of your fellow citizens, you can never regain their respect and esteem.

TRUTH

☞ I have faith in the people . . . let them know the truth and the country is safe.

UNION

☞ You can have no oath registered in heaven to destroy the government; while I shall have the most solemn one to "preserve, protect, and defend" it.

☞ The government must be preserved in spite of the acts of any man or set of men.

UNITY

☞ A house divided against itself cannot stand.†

☞ If all do not join now to save the good old ship of the Union this voyage, nobody will have a chance to pilot her on another voyage.

---

*A scrap of verse that Lincoln wrote as a young man.

†Lincoln reworded the biblical phrase "If a house be divided against itself, it cannot stand." MARK 3:25

URGENCY

☞ The necessity increases; look to it.*

VICES

☞ It has been my experience that folks who have no vices have very few virtues.

VICTORY

☞ Beware of rashness, but with energy and sleepless vigilance go forward and give us victories.†

☞ Wise councils may accelerate it or mistakenly delay it, but sooner or later the victory is sure to come.

☞ If we do not do right I believe God will let us go our own way to ruin. But if we do right, I believe He will lead us safely out of this wilderness, adorning our arms with victory.

VOTING

☞ Ballots are the rightful and peaceful successors of bullets.

WAR

☞ Military glory—that attractive rainbow that rises in showers of blood.

☞ I shall never live to see peace. This war is killing me.‡

---

*Lincoln's telegram to Governor Andrew Curtin in 1863.

†Telegram to General Joseph Hooker upon his assumption of the command of the Army of the Potomac.

‡Comment to Harriet Beecher Stowe in March 1865.

☞ War is most terrible and this of ours in its magnitude and duration is one of the most terrible the world has ever known.

WAR EXPLOITERS
☞ I wish that every one of them had their devilish head shot off.

WEALTH
☞ Wealth is a superfluity of things we don't need.

WOMEN
☞ If all that has been said by orators and poets—since the creation of the world—were applied to the women of America, it would not do the full justice for their conduct of the War. . . . God bless the women of America.

☞ Woman . . . the only thing I am afraid of that I know can't hurt me.

WOMEN'S SUFFRAGE
☞ I go for admitting all whites to the right of suffrage who pay taxes or bear arms (by no means excluding females).

WORK
☞ Wanting to work is so rare a merit that it should be continued.

YOUTH
☞ We have all heard of Young America. He is the most *current* youth of the age. Some think him conceited and arrogant. But has he not reason to entertain a rather extensive opinion of himself? Is

he not the inventor and owner of the *present* and sole hope of the *future*?

☞ You must not wait to be brought forward by the older men. For instance, do you suppose that I should have ever got into notice if I had waited to be hoisted up and pushed forward by older men?

☞ Young America is a great friend of humanity.

Lincoln Lore

From his birth in a log cabin to the martyrdom of his assassination, the life of Lincoln is the stuff of legend. Lincoln was both a lawyer and a professional politician—pursuits that are held in minimal esteem in today's world. Yet Lincoln's character stands in dramatic contrast to today's flamboyant trial lawyers and preening blow-dry-haired politicians. The very homeliness of Lincoln seems to suggest principles, honesty, and candor that the anchormen look-alikes of today's candidates lack.

Lincoln, unlike contemporary politicians, employed no speech-writer. When his Secretary of State-Designate William Seward handed him his draft for the inaugural address in 1861, Lincoln looked at it but then put it in his own words.

In a day when politicians seem obsessed with their image, the picture of the unkempt Lincoln is a wholesome contrast. Lack of pretense is a virtue rarely witnessed in today's media-conscious politicians.

It has been written that the Eastern establishment—the elite of the business, professional, and academic community—viewed Lincoln at first not unlike the way Lyndon Johnson was later regarded: as a gangly, crude politician from the West with a penchant for earthy humor. If Lincoln, however, approximated an LBJ at the time of inauguration, he would become almost a Christ-like figure after the assassination.

Whatever the closeness between Lincoln and Johnson physically, they were poles apart spiritually. Unlike LBJ, Lincoln possessed an innate humility. Lincoln's humility was rooted in an awareness of his and any man's limitations.

Even more fabled than Lincoln's modesty was his honesty. The story of his walking miles to return a few pennies to correct an overpayment is known to all. Such rectitude is a contrast to current congressional practices of accepting free air travel, padding their office expenses, and then pocketing campaign election funds when they retire. But more than Lincoln's impeccability in financial affairs, it was his integrity of character and ideals that made him a legend. Today politicians seem governed by the latest opinion polls. One changes his principles according to fashion as he would his ties. As Lincoln proved in his vote on the Mexican War, he would not compromise his belief. Despite popular support for the war, he argued that the war did not stem from Mexico's aggressive act.

If the log cabin birth and violent death frame his life, the warm colors of his honesty and humanity constitute the picture.

ə ə ə

BEDELL'S BEARD

Abraham Lincoln did not grow his famous beard until after he was nominated for the presidency in 1860. He was clean-shaven. During his campaign he received a letter from a little girl named Grace

Bedell, who lived in Westfield, New York. She wrote that she had seen his portrait and thought he would look better with whiskers. She promised that if he let his whiskers grow, she would try to persuade her older brothers, who were Democrats, to vote for him.

Lincoln wrote back to her on October 19, 1860:

Miss Grace Bedell,

My Dear Little Miss: Your very agreeable letter of the fifteenth is received. I regret the necessity of saying that I have no daughter. I have three sons: one seventeen, one nine, and one seven years of age. They, with their mother, constitute my whole family. As to the whiskers, having never worn any, do you not think people would call it a piece of silly affectation if I should begin it now?

Your very sincere well-wisher, A. Lincoln.

Lincoln, however, soon changed his mind on the subject. When he was on his way to Washington to be inaugurated, the train stopped at Westfield. Remembering young Grace Bedell, Lincoln inquired after her. It was soon discovered that she was present in the crowd. The President-Elect asked her to come forward so she might see that he had allowed his whiskers to grow at her request. She timidly obliged and he lifted her up and kissed her while the crowd roared its approval. He wore a beard ever after.

BOARDINGHOUSE BUDDY

In his one term in Congress, Lincoln struck up a friendship with another Whig lawyer named James Pollock. Pollock, who hailed from central Pennsylvania, shared lodging with Lincoln at Mrs. Spriggs's house a few blocks from the Capitol. Both Lincoln and

Pollock were opposed to the Mexican War, yet they knew that a negative vote on the war could abort their political careers. Night after night at the boardinghouse dinner, the two young representatives wrestled with the issue. They both decided to vote no.

On that issue Pollock was defeated for reelection. Lincoln, on the other hand, declined to run for reelection.

Lincoln went back to practicing law. Pollock, after his congressional defeat, was elected governor of Pennsylvania but then was defeated for his reelection in 1857.

When Lincoln became President, he appointed his old friend Pollock to be superintendent of the mint.

In March 1865 Superintendent Pollock came to the White House with an idea: to put an inscription *In God We Trust* on the nickel. Lincoln agreed and signed the executive order.

"CAPITAL" SENTIMENT

From Germany came a letter applauding Lincoln's reelection in November 1864:

> We congratulate you on your re-election by the American people. If resistance to slave power was the watchword of your first election in 1860, the triumphal war cry of your re-election is death to slavery.

The letter was signed by Karl Marx, who had recently published *Das Kapital*.

CAUGHT IN THE ACT

At the time of the first Republican convention in Philadelphia in 1856, Lincoln, who was following Judge Davis around the circuit in Illinois, was attending a special term of the court in Urbana. Judge

Davis, Lincoln, and other nonresident lawyers were quartered at the leading inn of the town.

The worst feature of the inn was the strident gong that summoned them to breakfast each morning. So they decided one day that the offending instrument must be removed or in some way forever silenced. By a majority vote Lincoln was chosen to carry out the decree.

Accordingly, a little earlier than usual before noon that day, he was seen to leave the courtroom and hasten to the hotel. Slipping unobserved into the dining room, he managed to secure the gong, secreted it under his coat, and was in the act of making off with it when Judge Davis suddenly appeared on the scene.

The Judge held in his hand a copy of the Chicago *Tribune,* which had just reached town. It contained the surprising and gratifying announcement that Mr. Lincoln had received 110 votes for Vice President at the Philadelphia convention the day before.

"Look at this larceny," Davis said with a chuckle, "for a man who aspires to be Vice President of the United States!"

CONSUMER PROTECTION

Lincoln's first salaried job was as clerk in a general store of New Salem. While tending shop one day, a woman put her money for the goods on the counter and left. As Lincoln gathered up the coins he realized the buyer had overpaid by 6½ cents. When the store closed for the day, Lincoln walked four miles to repay the shortchanged customer.

Many politicians before and since have advertised themselves as "honest." But for Lincoln, the sobriquet "Honest Abe" was rooted in truth.

DEAD DRUNK

On his way homeward with friends one winter night, young Lincoln discovered a riderless horse. After some looking around, they saw its owner sprawled nearby—lying passed out drunk. Though Lincoln's friends urged him to let the man be, Lincoln was afraid the besotted rider would not survive the cold night.

Lincoln picked him up and carried him to the nearest house. Then he stayed with him, telling his friends to get word to his father he would not be home that night. The next day the man—now recovered—thanked Lincoln for saving his life.

THE "DOGGEREL" DUEL

Did Lincoln fight a duel? The conflict was triggered by the publication of a humorous poem that ridiculed the amorous pretensions of a prominent Illinois politician, James Shields.

Even if the five-foot-one-inch height of Shields was hardly a heroic stature, he still pictured himself the answer to a young woman's dreams. One object of his attentions was Mary Owens, who did not concur in Shields's opinion of himself but was enamored of Lincoln. She and her girlfriend, in a giggly whim, composed a doggerel ditty that lampooned Shields, and then had it published in the Springfield paper.

An irate Shields called the editor and demanded the name of the author. The editor asked Lincoln what he should do and the gallant Lincoln replied, "Tell Shields I wrote them."

Thereupon, Shields challenged Lincoln to a duel. Under the dueling code the party challenged had the choice of weapons. Lincoln, who did not believe in dueling, tried to compel Shields to withdraw the challenge by proposing the most absurd conditions.

Since the long-legged and long-armed Lincoln of six-foot-four-inch height dwarfed the diminutive Shields, he proposed to Shields that they fight with broadswords on an island in the Mississippi River on some wooded planks. If one of the contestants retreated three feet back of the plank, he would lose.

Despite these impossible conditions for the short-armed Shields, he accepted. The contesting parties took a three-day ride to get to the island. On the plank just before the contest, Lincoln reached with his saber and cut off a twig which no one else could have reached.

The actual fight did not take place. The supporters of Lincoln treated it as a joke as Shields tried to maintain that a cowardly Lincoln withdrew.

Shields later would become a Civil War general and U.S. senator. Mary Owen and Lincoln would break off their engagement.

DROP IN THE HAT

In 1832 Lincoln assumed the nonpaying duties of New Salem postmaster because it enabled him to read all the newspapers and magazines that came to the office. When the occasion demanded that Lincoln leave the office, he would leave his hat, in which customers could drop their mail.

"DRUM" MAJOR

When war broke out in April 1861, states were reluctant to dispatch their volunteer state militia units for federal use in defense of the nation's capital. The populous state of Pennsylvania, whose capital, Harrisburg, was less than a hundred miles from Washington, was no exception.

Lincoln asked A. H. McClure, a loyal political ally from Philadelphia, to help expedite matters.

"Mr. President," reported McClure on his trip to the Pennsylvania capital, "I can't shake Harrisburg loose."

"What's the rank of the officer in Harrisburg holding it up?" asked Lincoln.

"Captain," answered McClure.

Lincoln then said to his military aide, "Get the adjutant general here." (The adjutant general was the army's federal army chief officer and was the liaison for all state militias.)

When the adjutant general arrived, Lincoln said to him, "Swear in McClure as assistant adjutant general with rank of major."

"But, Mr. President," protested McClure, "I don't want to serve the army."

"You won't except for a couple days. Just enough to go to Harrisburg and back."

"Major" McClure went straightaway to Harrisburg. To the recalcitrant captain, McClure brandished his commission that outranked the Pennsylvania officer. The result was that troops followed McClure back to Washington. Then McClure resigned his commission.

EVIL

The story has been told how Lincoln in his first trip to New Orleans saw a young octoroon woman being auctioned off to the highest male bidder.

The nineteen-year-old Lincoln was revolted by the sight. As his cousin Dennis Hanks later reported, Lincoln said, "By God, boys, if I ever get a chance to hit that thing, I'll hit it and hit it hard."

EXTENSION OF CREDIT

President Lincoln was always careful to give credit to his generals for any victories that were achieved.

Soon after the Battle of Gettysburg, Lincoln sensed an opportunity to end the war by driving hard against Lee's rear in retreat. As commander in chief he ordered General George G. Meade to pursue. He attached the following handwritten note along with the official orders: "The order I enclose is not of record. If you succeed, you need not publish the order. If you fail, publish it. Then if you succeed, you will have all the credit of the movement. If not, I'll take the responsibility."

FAIR GAME?

A potential client came into Lincoln's Springfield law office. He wanted to retain Lincoln's services to attach the property of a widow to collect in damages what the husband had owed him in a contractual dispute.

Lincoln listened and said: "I know I can win your case for you. But at what price? I can distress a widowed mother and her six fatherless children, and thereby gain for you six hundred dollars. I shall not take your case, but I will give you a little advice for nothing. You seem an industrious and enterprising man. I would advise you to try your hand at making six hundred dollars in some other way."

FAME OR FORTUNE

Mrs. Lincoln may have had her detractors, but the short, buxom Mary Todd saw early in the awkward, ungainly state legislator what many missed. The vivacious Mary Todd was the belle of the Springfield society. She attracted many suitors—all of them with more wealth and family credentials than Lincoln. Her callers included none other than Stephen Douglas.

At one soiree Mary Todd was asked by a woman friend why she gave the cold shoulder to a rich gentleman visitor.

"I'd rather marry a good man, a man of mind and bright prospects for fame and power than all the gold stones in the world."

FEE REFUSED

A woman called on Lincoln to represent her in a suit for damages. A few days later she returned to Lincoln's Springfield office.

"Ma'am," said Lincoln, "I can't find a peg on which would enable you to win."

She nodded and handed him a check for $250.

Lincoln handed it back saying, "I can't take pay for doing my duty."

FIRM HAND

On New Year's Day 1863, President Lincoln hosted a large reception at the Executive Mansion. It was to mark his signing of the Emancipation Proclamation. After shaking hands with visitors for two hours, the weary Lincoln sat down. Soon the time came for Lincoln to sign the proclamation. Lincoln, however, delayed. An aide asked him what was the problem. "After all that shaking of hands mine seem to be trembling a bit," Lincoln replied. "But I didn't want to sign with 'shaky' signature and let the nation think I was hesitant about this proclamation."

THE FIRST ELECTION

When the Black Hawk War [an Indian uprising] erupted in 1832, Lincoln left his store, borrowed a horse, and rode to Richmond Creek to enlist in the local militia. After all the recruits took their oath, the company was called upon to elect their captain. Immediately three-quarters of the unit stepped out to place themselves by Lincoln. Then one by one the others followed.

Lincoln would later write that he "was surprised" and "not since—had any success in life that gave me so much satisfaction."

FOR HEAVEN'S SAKE?

A wife of a Confederate officer imprisoned in Tennessee called on President Lincoln to request that her husband be chosen for exchange.

"Mr. Lincoln," she implored, "my husband is a devout Christian."

"Really!" was Lincoln's dry response.

"Oh yes," she expounded, "he prays twice a day."

"Twice a day," echoed Lincoln.

"Mr. Lincoln," she continued, "I want you to know my husband is a deeply religious man."

Lincoln answered, "You say your husband is a religious man; tell him when you see him that I said I am not much of a judge of religion, but that, in my opinion, the religion that sets men to rebel and fight against their government, because as they think, that government does not sufficiently help some men to eat their bread in the sweat of other men's faces is not the sort of religion upon which people can get to heaven!"

HANDY ANDY

Hannibal Hamlin served as Vice President during Lincoln's first term. The former senator from Maine got on amicably with Lincoln. Yet Lincoln decided to dump Hamlin as his running mate in his reelection campaign in 1864.

His choice to replace Hamlin was Andrew Johnson of Tennessee. Tennessee had rejoined the Union in 1864 and had elected Johnson as its governor.

A. H. McClure, a staunch political friend of Lincoln in Pennsylvania, was asked by the President to nominate Johnson.

"I'll do it if you request it," muttered McClure. "But, why Johnson? He's a Democrat and he's not liked by a lot of people, including me."

"McClure," said Lincoln, "we are trying to stave off recognition of the Confederacy by Britain as well as France. They don't really understand what the number-two man in our government does. If we have Johnson, a Democrat from a Southern state as Vice President, we are proving that the South is coming back to the Union and a Southerner as Vice President shows that our country is not just a Northern government but a national administration."

"HANG IT ALL!"

Lincoln relished his years in the state legislature in Springfield. He thought Congress and Washington would be just the same but at a higher level. But he found Congress uncongenial and unfriendly to a freshman member. He wrote back to a friend: "I feel like the boy whose teacher asked him why he did not spell better. The boy answered, ' 'Cause I hain't just got the hang of the schoolhouse but I'll get better later on.'"

HANK'S PLANKS

Even though Lincoln was born in a log cabin, that campaign symbol had already been exploited by General Harrison's winning presidential campaign in 1840. (Even if the Virginia aristocrat had actually been born in a Tidewater mansion.)

Those handling the Lincoln campaign in 1860 for nomination were dispatched to his home environs to dig out material. When Lincoln's cousin Denny Hanks related to Republican politicians how he and Abe had "split rails together," the campaign handlers asked if he could locate any of them.

Hanks managed to find some, and so hundreds of those wood planks were taken to the Republican convention in Chicago.

There at the "Wigwam," the city convention hall, the rails were mounted in an exhibition framed by red, white, and blue bunting. At night, candles lit up the log ties underneath two crossed sledge-hammers.

When a reporter asked Lincoln if these were actually the planks he once split to make rails, he cautiously allowed, "Well, they sure look like them."

Such was the source of the sobriquet, "Abe Lincoln, the Rail Splitter." These planks were then sold off around the country to county organizations to raise funds for the Republican presidential campaign in 1860.

HAPPY LANDING

In December 1859, Lincoln was walking back from the State House in Springfield after the legislators narrowly elected Stephen Douglas as the U.S. senator. On the snowy road to his house, suddenly he came upon an icy patch. Though his body spun, he managed to keep his feet.

When he got home, he told his wife that his near tumble in a way described what happened in the Senate election. "I had a slip not a fall."

In an election where Lincoln actually outpolled Douglas with the Illinois voters, he had not failed. In fact, with the national prominence he had gained, Lincoln's political future was brighter than ever.

HAT TRICK

Lincoln's silk stovepipe hat was part of his office. It served as his desk when he would jot notes on its flat top and also his file drawer where he would keep his datebook, checkbook, and letters. When he would think of an idea, he would scribble it on a piece of paper and then insert it in the hatband.

"HOUSE" PARTY

Lincoln had few occasions for celebrating in his early manhood. But he did allow himself to be treated by his political supporters when he won his seat to the Illinois Legislature in 1834 at the age of twenty-five.

Had he lost instead of won, the world might have gained a surveyor or even a blacksmith and lost a President. The store that he half owned had gone under. He was heavily in debt, and one unreasonable creditor had attached his horse and surveying instruments for debt—literally snatching the bread out of his mouth. The $4 a day which Illinois legislators then received must have seemed manna from heaven. It also signaled a new future for Lincoln—first as a legislator then as a lawyer.

Intellectually, the legislature removed him at once from the dull routine of village life to the companionship and rivalry of the keenest minds gathered from all parts of the state. It taxed all his knowledge, and confronted him with new and absorbing problems, leading him to the practice of law.

THE "KNOW-NOTHING" CANARD

The Know-Nothing party received its name because its adherents, when asked about their beliefs, stated, "I know nothing."

In 1856, when they ran former President Millard Fillmore for President, the Know-Nothings adopted the official party name of "Native American." The term was suggestive of their opposition to immigration of anybody but white European Protestants. Yet, the Know-Nothings were no friends of the slave South, for they opposed the extension of slavery to the Territories.

In the 1860 presidential campaign, Lincoln's enemies spread the rumor that he had been a secret lodge member in Illinois of the Know-Nothings. A Jewish supporter of Lincoln, Abraham Jonas, wrote to ask the Republican presidential candidate to dispel the charges.

The facts were that Lincoln ten years earlier had denounced the Know-Nothings as violating the Declaration of Independence. Yet Lincoln in 1860 did not want to attack publicly the Know-Nothings, since it could drive them to support Douglas. After all, since the Know-Nothings opposed the extension of slavery, they were probably leaning in favor of Lincoln.

In his response to Jonas, Lincoln denied that he ever attended a Know-Nothing lodge meeting and told him to relay that message

to his friends. Lincoln viewed the rumor as concocted and spread by
Democrats to force Lincoln to attack the Know-Nothings.

LINCOLN FOR VICE PRESIDENT?

In early 1856, Lincoln left the Whig party to become a
Republican. He addressed a meeting in Bloomington, Illinois, that
gave birth to the state's Republican party. His opposition to Senator
Douglas's Kansas-Nebraska Act triggered the first mention of his
name outside of Illinois.

Still, Lincoln passed up the chance to attend the first Republican
presidential convention in Philadelphia that May. If Lincoln had
gone to the convention, he conceivably could have been on the
national Republican ticket four years earlier than he was.

Even in his absence Lincoln's name was considered as a vice presidential possibility. But it was William Dayton of New Jersey who
was selected, although Lincoln did come in second with 110 votes.

At any rate, in 1856—unlike four years later—the Republican
ticket led by explorer John C. Fremont had little chance. Their slogan, though, was a winner: "Free Men, Free Soil, and Fremont."

THE LINCOLN LEAP

In 1836, the Democratic-controlled Illinois legislature would not
raise the revenue to enable the state to redeem its bonds. The
Democrats wanted to embarrass the banks and their Whig friends in
the business community. Under state law, default would be incurred
if the legislature adjourned without action.

The minority-party Whigs led by Lincoln tried to prevent
adjournment by denying the quorum necessary to vote for adjournment. On one fateful afternoon, the Democratic speaker, who was

presiding while Lincoln was addressing the House, realized that the presence of Lincoln and a few of his fellow Whigs constituted a quorum. He quickly had a vote for adjournment called.

Lincoln quickly sensed the situation and leaped out the State House window.

A LITTLE WOMAN

Abraham Lincoln was sitting in the newspaper office of the *State Journal* in Springfield, Illinois, when the news arrived from the local telegraph office across the street that he had been nominated for President by the Republican party at its convention in Chicago.

"Mr. Lincoln, you are nominated on the third ballot," the telegraph operator wrote on a scrap of paper.

Amid the tumultuous shouts and cheers of his friends all around him, Lincoln stared at the piece of paper silently. Then Lincoln rose, tucked the piece of paper into his pocket, and said quietly, "There's a little woman down at our house who would like to hear this. I'll go down and tell her."

LONELY HEART

During the Civil War, President Lincoln was besieged with appeals for pardons for soldiers caught in the machinery of military discipline. Such appeals were usually supported by letters from influential people. One day Lincoln found on his desk a single sheet of paper—an appeal from a Union army private without any supporting documents.

"What? Has this man no friends?" exclaimed the President.

"No sir," said the adjutant, "not one."

Lincoln sighed. "Then I will be his friend."

MARRY MARY?

The courtship of Mary Todd by Lincoln was anything but smooth. Lincoln was at first meeting attracted to the short and buxom Mary, whose vivacity and wit made her Springfield's most sought-after belle. The Todds, who were an old established family— counting senators and generals as kin—thought Mary could make a better match than the ungainly and unwealthy Lincoln. Mary, however, saw greatness in the struggling lawyer.

Yet it was Lincoln who broke off the engagement because he feared marriage to anyone. A depressed Lincoln withdrew into a period of melancholy. Mary Todd, however, did not rage at the rejection but bided her time.

Months later a new date for marriage was set. And Lincoln purchased a wedding ring and ordered this inscription: "Love is Eternal."

MISSING MATE?

The Republican party convention in Chicago nominated Abraham Lincoln of Illinois for President and Senator Hannibal Hamlin from Maine for Vice President. Lincoln did not attend the proceeding, but closely monitored the various ballots which culminated in his nomination in the cable office at Springfield.

Lincoln accepted the nomination, but over the summer he had not heard from his running mate. So Lincoln sent Hamlin the following note:

Hon. Hannibal Hamlin,

My Dear Sir: It appears to me that you and I ought to be acquainted, and accordingly I write this as a sort of introduction of myself to you.

You first entered the Senate during the single term I was a member of the House of Representatives, but I have no recollection that we were introduced. I shall be pleased to receive a line from you.

The prospect of Republican success now appears very flattering, so far as I can perceive. Do you see anything to the contrary?

Yours truly, A. Lincoln

MOONLIGHT MURDER?

In 1857 Lincoln was at the top of the legal profession, making a handsome living—mostly in railroad litigation. Yet suddenly he interrupted his civil practice for a case in criminal court. A son of his old friend Jack Armstrong was charged with murder.

Despite the fact that the Armstrong family had no money with which to retain a lawyer, Lincoln agreed to represent Duff Armstrong.

The alleged murder took place following a campfire meeting. The strongest evidence against Duff Armstrong was an eyewitness who claimed to have seen the defendant strike the victim with a slingshot. In cross-examination of the chief witness, Lincoln asked how, at a distance of 150 feet at eleven o'clock at night, he could describe the weapon and the killing with such detail.

The witness replied, "It was a bright moon—a full moon."

After putting the witness on record, Lincoln then produced an almanac which said that on August 29—the date in question—the moon was barely past the fourth quarter and that it actually had disappeared by eleven o'clock. When Lincoln destroyed the credibility of the key witness, he won the acquittal of Duff Armstrong.

"NO HIT" PITCHER

Edward Baker, who preceded Lincoln to Congress, was Lincoln's close friend. In fact, Lincoln's son was named for him. Once, Edward Baker, noted for his diatribes, attacked a local newspaper before an audience of voters. It took place immediately beneath the office of Stuart and Lincoln. Lincoln lay listening on the second floor through a trapdoor that separated the two floors.

"Get him!" shouted the brother of the newspaper editor, and for a moment it looked rather ominous for Baker. The crowd advanced, when to their astonishment the lank form of Lincoln, feet first, started to dangle to the room below. Gesturing in vain for silence, Lincoln seized the water pitcher and shouted, "I'll break it over the head of the first man who tries to hit Baker!"

And then he continued, "Gentlemen, this is a land where freedom of speech is guaranteed. Mr. Baker has a right to speak and no man shall take him from this stand if I can prevent him." And order was restored.

"NO NEWS IS GOOD NEWS"

Lincoln as a state legislator wrote to a friend in Chicago what it was like in New Salem.

"We generally have in this [Sangamon] County—Peace, Health, Plenty and No News."

NO SINGLE SHINGLE

On the day before Abraham Lincoln left on the train that would eventually take him to Washington to be inaugurated as President, he sat down with his young partner Billy Herndon to go over matters of business. After they had finished their talk, Lincoln threw himself down on the old lounge, and for a while neither spoke. Then Lincoln began to recount some of the funny things while riding circuit in his legal career. Herndon, who was the partner who stayed back in Springfield to mind the store, enjoyed listening to tales of Lincoln's trials.

It was only as Lincoln was taking his leave that he paused on the threshold and, with a sudden change of tone, asked that the office sign LINCOLN AND HERNDON be allowed to hang undisturbed. "Give our clients to understand that the election of a President makes no difference," he said. "If I live I'm coming back sometime, and we'll go right on practicing law, as if nothing had happened."

NO WILDERNESS WIFE!

In 1848, after his unpopular vote against President Polk's Mexican War, Congressman Lincoln decided not to run for reelection. Instead, he threw his efforts into campaigning in Illinois for the Whig presidential candidate, Zachary Taylor.

General Taylor, the hero of the Mexican War, won. Illinois was one of the key states he carried.

In winding up his congressional career in Washington, Lincoln stayed around to press for a top political appointment. He had now given up any ambition in elective politics.

Lincoln first aimed for the key job of Commissioner of the Land Office, but was rebuffed. Then he was offered the governorship of the Oregon Territory.

Lincoln was all set to move to the Oregon Territory, but Mrs. Lincoln was dead set against moving from Illinois. She told Lincoln, "I won't ever live in any wilderness."

If Lincoln had not acquiesced to his wife's wishes, he never would have been elected to the presidency.

"OLD BUCK" PASSES THE BUCK

As the term of the fifteenth President wound down to its end, James Buchanan wrestled with the insurmountable problem of avoiding war. Many of his own cabinet members were open Southern sympathizers.

"Old Buck," as Buchanan was once affectionately referred to by his friends, had expected his presidential term to cap a distinguished career in public service—as senator, secretary of state, and minister to the Court of St. James in London. Instead, he found his reputation crumbling in the final year of his term. The ordeal had visibly aged Buchanan.

As Buchanan rode down in the presidential carriage from the Executive Mansion to the Capitol for the inauguration ceremonies, he said to President-elect Lincoln:

"If you are as happy coming into this office, as I am in leaving it, you are the happiest man in America."

"OUT, OUT, BRIEF CANDLE . . . "

Abraham Lincoln kept four books on his White House desk: the U.S. Constitution, a copy of the U.S. Statutes, the King James version of the Bible, and a collection of Shakespeare's tragedies.

Lincoln had been first introduced to Shakespeare by a New Salem character, Jack Kelso. To some he was a town drunk, but to others who would listen, such as Lincoln, he was a walking repository of Shakespeare's dramatic verse as well as Robert Burns's ballads, which he would recite to any audience who would listen.

Kelso whetted Lincoln's interest in Shakespeare. He especially loved the Bard's tragedies. His favorite was *Macbeth*.

A few days before his fateful trip to Ford's Theater, Lincoln was heard in the White House reciting aloud that haunting soliloquy by the Scottish king:

> *Out, out, brief candle! Life's but a walking shadow—a poor player who struts and frets his hour upon the stage and then is heard no more. 'Tis a tale told by an idiot full of sound and fury signifying nothing.*

A PATENT SUCCESS

The only President to have registered a patent for an invention was Abraham Lincoln. In 1849, Lincoln received a patent for his invention for adjustable buoyant chambers for steamboats. This device enabled large ships to navigate in shallow waters—even canals. As one who all his life lived in the country of the Mississippi and its tributaries, Lincoln had witnessed all the labor and time entailed in transferring loads from larger to smaller craft. This adjustable chamber allowed boats to alter their draft in water.

PAYBACK

Although Lincoln only had a few years of education, he tried to expand his learning by reading any book he could lay his hands on. At age fourteen he heard that a neighboring farmer had a copy of Mason Weems's *Life of George Washington* (the biography that popularized the apocryphal cherry tree incident). Lincoln borrowed and then read and reread it for weeks—sometimes by candlelight into the night. To his chagrin, he woke up one morning to find that a

The Wit & Wisdom of Abraham Lincoln LINCOLN LORE

thunderstorm during the night had seeped in between the logs of the cabin and wet the pages.

Lincoln told what happened to the owner. The neighbor said that he had purchased the book at $2.50 and that Lincoln could repay the debt by three days of work cleaning out the cornstalks of his field. In a feverish spate of energy, Lincoln did it in two days. In the cornfield not a blade was left on a stalk.

Said Lincoln afterwards:

"I wanted to pay in full and fast. The result was a quick clean sweep."

PLATFORM PROFILES

Those who gathered at the Capitol for the March 4 inauguration ceremony of the sixteenth President were struck by four figures on the platform before the Capitol steps.

One was the outgoing President Buchanan. In 1861, Buchanan was the oldest man to have presided over the nation. Yet Buchanan looked even older than his sixty-seven years. With his hair now white and his frame bent, his body testified to the ordeal of the last trying months. Still his face beamed the signs of relief from the care of office.

Next to Buchanan was Chief Justice Roger Taney, a short wizened old man. Taney, a Marylander and slaveholder, was a Southern sympathizer who, four years before, had handed down the Dred Scott decision—the "fugitive slave" ruling that had split the nation in controversy. Taney looked sour. He was about to administer the oath of office to a new President whose political policies he despised.

On the left side of the President sat the man whom Lincoln had defeated—Stephen Douglas. Douglas's full face bore a bemused grin at the political fates which awarded his fellow Illinoisan the prize he had always sought. Ironically, his senatorial victory over Lincoln in 1859 had propelled his erstwhile opponent to the national prominence that led to the Republican's recent presidential victory.

The object of greatest interest to the Washington crowd was, of course, the newly whiskered six-foot-four President-elect, who towered over the rest of the platform dignitaries. For many, this was their first glimpse of the Western lawyer, whom his campaign pamphlets had called the "Rail-Splitter."

RED TAPE CUTTER

An aide entered to find the President counting greenbacks.

"What are you doing?" asked the astonished aide.

"A porter at the Treasury Department is laid up with smallpox," Lincoln explained. "He is owed back wages, so I am what you call 'cutting through all the red tape' to give what's his due."

RESIDENT RUBE

In 1856, Lincoln was retained as a resident attorney when John Manning, Inc., an engineering company, sued the Cyrus McCormick Corporation for patent infringement.

In order to bring the suit in Illinois, Manning had to have a local attorney "of record." Lincoln, despite his success as a trial lawyer, was relegated to a nominal position in the case. The Eastern lawyer took one look at the lanky, unkempt Lincoln with the hick accent and assessed that he could be of little assistance.

Little did Edwin Stanton realize that one day that country lawyer would be his boss when he would be Lincoln's Secretary of War.

THE RICHMOND REDEEMER

The first positive proof that the Civil War had ended was a wire from Richmond, the capital of the Confederacy, saying that the Confederate officials and army had abandoned the city.

While Stanton, Lincoln's Secretary of War, was away visiting troops, Lincoln ignored Stanton's recommendations and decided to visit Richmond. When his steamship landed at the Richmond harbor, he made his way to the town, only to find he was mobbed by former slaves who recognized him and fell on their knees before him, exclaiming their thanks over their deliverance.

Besides "Mr. President," some of the other phrases of address were "Savior" and "Redeemer."

Lincoln answered their cries with an order: "Don't kneel to me—it isn't right!"

"You must kneel to God only," he continued, "and thank Him for the liberty you now enjoy. I am but God's humble instrument but you may rest assured, that as long as I live, you shall have all the rights which God has given to every other free citizen of the Republic."

RUDE RUFFIANS

A trio of young roughnecks entered Lincoln's New Salem general store. Their foul language offended Lincoln—particularly when they made obscene remarks to a woman shopper who came by. Finally, Lincoln said to the ringleader, "If you must be whipped, I suppose I may as well whip you as any other man." And he did.

SCHOOL OF "HAPPY" KNOCKS

In 1864, Robert Lincoln, the President's eldest, graduated from

Harvard. He desperately wanted to enlist, but Lincoln, because of his wife's tearful demands, would not let him.

In a talk at the Executive Mansion, Lincoln asked his son what he planned to do.

"Well," replied Robert, "if I can't go into the army, I'll go back to Harvard one more year and study law."

Lincoln, who never went to college and got his legal education by clerking for another lawyer and studying at night, replied, "If you do, you should learn more than I ever did, but you would never have such a good time."

SCRAPBOOK SENTENCES

In a leather-covered scrapbook, six by four inches in size, with a brass clasp, Lincoln pasted the Declaration of Independence paragraph declaring "all men created equal," followed by two passionate sentences from Henry Clay of Kentucky. "I repeat it, sir, I never can, and never will, and no earthly power will make me vote, directly or indirectly, to spread slavery over territory where it does not exist. Never, while my heart sends the vital fluid through my veins— never!"

STARS IN YOUR EYES

During the darker days of the Civil War, Lincoln was asked by some White House visitors how to react to the latest defeat. He told of an overnight trip he took on a forest ridge with a youth—in the middle of the night a shower of meteors fell that frightened the lad.

Lincoln had said, "Son, don't look at the shooting stars—keep your eyes on the fixed stars—the sky—that have guided us in the past."

"Gentlemen," he concluded, "we must be ever guided by the idea our forefathers set before us."

STATELY CANT VS. HOMELY TRUTH

The Lincoln-Douglas Debates are a singular spectacle in American politics—the clash of principles on an issue that would trigger the most bloody rift in American history.

Stephen Douglas, the most famous political name on the American scene, advocated his cause of "popular sovereignty." His challenger Abraham Lincoln countered that the Douglas solution opened up the possibility of slavery in the Territories. Their differences were accentuated by their contrast in styles.

Douglas was all of five-two. But his presence of the Little Grant was that of a titan. His baritone of sonorous elegance combined with theatrical gesture and actor's timing could mesmerize audiences.

His challenger towered over him at six feet four, yet his reedy drawl was more that of a farmer than orator. Lincoln was matter-of-fact, not majestic; anecdotal, not rhetorical.

Lincoln explained his position as he would to a backwoods jury, while Douglas exhorted as he would to a Senate chamber.

Their delivery was no less a contrast than their dress. The short Douglas was tailored like a Southern planter—a white three-vested suit with gold chain, compared with the lanky Lincoln, whose black unpressed suit ill-fit his gawky frame.

Douglas would come to an Illinois town for the debate in a handsomely appointed private car of a train with a cannon on top to announce his arrival. Unheralded, Lincoln would enter the same town more often as not on the same train as just another paying passenger.

But if Lincoln lost in the state legislature, his folksy reasoning won more votes than Douglas's rehearsed phrases.

STEALTH OF THE NIGHT

While Lincoln was en route to Washington for his inauguration, both the U.S. Secret Service and private detectives discovered what they believed was a plot to assassinate him as he passed through Baltimore.

In alarm, Lincoln's friends pleaded with him to slip into Washington incognito by night.

Lincoln was decidedly against it. But finally, after insistent pleading, he bowed to the wishes of his trusted advisers.

It had been announced that Lincoln would speak in Harrisburg, Pennsylvania, on February 22, spend the night there, and then leave the next morning for Baltimore and Washington.

He made his speech in Harrisburg according to schedule; but instead of spending the night there, he slipped out of the back door of the hotel that evening at six and, disguised in an old threadbare overcoat and a soft wool hat such as he had never worn before, Lincoln was driven to an unlit railway coach. A few minutes later, an engine was whirling him away to Philadelphia, and the telegraph wires in Harrisburg were cut at once so that the information would not be relayed to the would-be assassins.

At Philadelphia, the Lincoln party had to wait for an hour to change trains and stations. In order to prevent recognition during that time, Lincoln and Allan Pinkerton, the famous detective, drove through the streets of the city in a darkened cab.

At 10:55 P.M., leaning on Pinkerton's arm and stooping so as not to draw attention to his height, Lincoln entered the station by a side door. He carried his head bent forward and had his old traveling shawl drawn close so that it almost covered his face. In that guise, he crossed the waiting room and made his way to the rear section of the last sleeping car on the train, which one of Pinkerton's aides, a woman, had cut off from the rest of the car by a heavy curtain and reserved for her "invalid brother."

In the early hours of February 23, the train carrying the President-elect arrived in Washington and Lincoln was met and taken unobserved to the Willard Hotel.

"STOOP TO CONQUER"

At an official reception during the Civil War, President Lincoln made a brief speech in which he referred to the Confederates as "erring human beings" rather than as enemies to be destroyed.

An elderly lady abolitionist said, "Mr. President, how can you lower yourself to refer to such slave holding rebels as merely 'erring human beings' who were sworn enemies to the Union and freedom?"

"Why, madam," replied Lincoln, "do I not destroy my enemies when I make them friends?"

STUCK PIG

For his law cases on the circuit court of Illinois, Lincoln purchased a new suit. Smartly attired, the lawyer began his horseback ride to the court session miles away when his thoughts were interrupted by a squealing pig.

Lincoln alit from his horse to discover a pig trapped in a hole. Though he pondered the risk of getting his new suit soiled, he nevertheless found some railroad ties and reached down the hole, positioning them so the trapped pig could maneuver its way out. When the pig climbed to safety, a dirty and disheveled Lincoln resumed his ride.

SWEET AND SIMPLE

The government printer, whose name was Morris Defrees, was disturbed by the President's use of colloquialisms in his message to Congress. Particularly objectionable to Defrees was Lincoln's use of the term *sugar-coated*.

"Sir," said Defrees, who was encouraged by Lincoln to speak freely, "a message to Congress is quite another matter from a speech at a mass meeting in Illinois. Your messages to Congress become a part of history and should be written accordingly."

"What is the matter this time?" asked the President.

"In your message you have used an undignified expression." He read aloud the paragraph in which the term *sugar-coated* occurred. "I would amend the structure of that, if I were you."

Lincoln shook his head. "Defrees," he said, "that word expresses precisely my idea, and I am not going to change it. The time will never come in this country when people won't know exactly what 'sugar-coated' means."

"TALL AND SMALL"

On one occasion when a crowd of well-wishers came to the back of the White House to express their support, the President asked his wife to appear with him on the second-story balcony. The petite and plump First Lady made quite a contrast to the lean and lanky President. Lincoln's words were, "Here am I and there's Mrs. Lincoln and that's the long and short of it."

THANKSGIVING DAY

The first time the nation ever officially celebrated Thanksgiving Day was in the autumn of 1864. On October 20, President Lincoln issued an official proclamation for a Thanksgiving observance on the fourth Thursday of November:

It has pleased Almighty God to prolong our national life another year, defending us with his guardian care against unfriendly designs from abroad and vouchsafing to us in His mercy many and signal victories over the enemy, who is of our own household. It has also pleased our Heavenly Father to favor as well our citizens in their homes as our sol-diers in their camps and our sailors on the rivers and seas with unusual health. He has largely augmented our free population by emancipation and by immigration, while he has opened to us new sources of wealth, and has crowned the labor of our working men in every department of industry with abundant rewards. Moreover, He has been pleased to ani-mate and inspire our minds and hearts with fortitude, courage, and res-olution sufficient for the great trial of civil war into which we have been brought by our adherence as a nation to the cause of Freedom and Humanity, and to afford to us reasonable hopes of an ultimate and happy deliverance from all our dangers and afflictions.

THE THREE B'S

A friend of Lincoln's reported that three works were the source of his wisdom. The Bible, Lincoln had told him, answered all questions about God and man's purpose in life. A mastering of Blackstone and his *Commentaries,* Lincoln had told him, were at the core of a lawyer's practice. Finally, Shakespeare, said Lincoln, offered the most pro-found insights into human nature.

The Bible, Blackstone, and the Bard represented the three works that shaped Lincoln's life, career, philosophy, and literary style.

"THREE LITTLE KITTENS . . ."

Once while visiting the army's telegraph hut in Washington, the President came across three lost kittens. He picked up one of the mewing kittens and said, "Where's your mother?"

An officer overhearing Lincoln said, "Sir, the mother is dead."

"Well," said Lincoln, stroking the kitty, "she can't grieve as many a poor mother is mourning for a son lost in battle."

Gathering the other kittens in his lap, he petted them and said gently, "Kittens, thank God you are cats and can't understand the terrible strife going on."

Then he turned to the officer in charge. "See that these poor little motherless waifs are given plenty of milk and treated kindly."

The hand that had recently signed the Emancipation Proclamation turned to caressing three stray kittens.

TOO BIG A BAR TAB

As a lawyer, Lincoln was a poor moneymaker. Daniel Webster, who sent him a case, was amazed at the smallness of his bill, and his fellow lawyers looked upon his fees as too low. This was Lincoln's only fault, in their eyes. Once, when another attorney had collected $250 for their joint services, Lincoln refused to accept his share until the fee had been reduced to what he considered fair proportions and the overcharge had been returned to the client. When Judge Davis, the presiding judge of the circuit, heard of this, he indignantly exclaimed, "Lincoln, your picayune charges will impoverish the bar."

UNDAUNTED

In 1832, Abraham Lincoln, then a twenty-three-year-old grocery clerk, ran for the state legislature. He was overwhelmingly defeated. The next year he became a partner in the general store. It went bankrupt.

In 1834, Lincoln, however, did win a state legislative seat. Yet in 1838, he would fail in his bid to be elected speaker.

In 1843, Lincoln sought the Whig party nomination for Congress. He lost. Three years later, in 1846, he gained the nomination and won the general election.

Lincoln did not seek reelection after his two-year term, knowing he would face certain defeat after opposing the Mexican War.

In 1855—as a candidate of the Republican party—he failed in his bid to be elected U.S. senator.

The next year he came in second at the Republican convention in the nomination as the party's vice presidential candidate.

Four years later, in 1859, he ran again for the U.S. Senate seat. He lost again to Stephen Douglas.

The next year, 1860, he was elected President.

WINNING IN THE STRETCH

Lincoln was once driving a two-horse team on a road heavy with mud. It was evening and Lincoln had his back to the sunset. And he met another driver with a two-horse wagon. Both knew that whoever turned aside would be up to the hubs in mud, almost sure to get mired.

"Turn aside," the other fellow called.

"Turn aside yourself," called Lincoln. The other fellow refused.

Then, with his back to the sunset, Lincoln began to stretch from his seat in the wagon—rising and rising. His long profile getting taller and taller against the setting sun, Lincoln said, "If you don't turn out I'll tell you what I'll do."

And the other fellow hollered, "Don't go any higher. I'll turn out." And after he had struggled through and passed by Lincoln, he called back, "Say, what would you have done if I hadn't turned aside?"

Lincoln answered, "I'd have turned aside myself."

WINNING TICKETS?

Although the 1860 Republican convention was meeting in Lincoln's home state of Illinois, those running the Chicago convention were friendly to Senator William Seward of New York, the leading candidate and most widely known Republican in the country. Lincoln's strategy was to attack none of the other candidates—Salmon Chase of Ohio, Edward McLean of Missouri, as well as Seward—so as to position himself as everyone's second choice.

If Lincoln was generally successful in making no enemies in pre-convention maneuvering, not much enthusiasm was kindled for Lincoln himself.

Lincoln had legions of supporters in Illinois, but the convention chairman had allotted the Lincoln home-state partisans relatively few gallery seats in the "Wigwam" convention hall.

Lincoln's managers overcame that by printing up forged tickets. The Lincoln supporters armed with the counterfeit tickets shook the hall with cheers as the votes for Lincoln rose with each ballot and launched the bandwagon to victory.

WITCH HUNT?

"Witch" was only one of the ugly epithets hurled at President Lincoln's wife. Mary Todd Lincoln was the object of a scurrilous rumor attack. Enemies of Lincoln spread tales that Mrs. Lincoln was a Southern sympathizer spy! After all, weren't her Todd kin rebels in the Confederate Army?

Mrs. Lincoln's compulsive spending binges lent ammunition to Lincoln's foes. Although Lincoln's presidency was ridiculed by the radical wing of congressional Republicans and their allies in the financial community and press, still the folksy and unpretentious Lincoln evoked an affectionate chords of empathy from working folk and their sons wearing Union Blue.

A congressional committee spotlighted the extravagant expenditures of the President's wife incurred in redecorating the Executive Mansion.

Mrs. Lincoln was the only First Lady ever to be subpoenaed by Congress. Even if nothing illegal was ultimately determined by the interrogation, the reports of Mrs. Lincoln's expensive tastes in furnishing—as well as her weakness for imported gowns and gloves— did not sit well with those families making sacrifices for the war. The crescendos of attacks on his wife pained an already burdened President.

Assassination Secrets

If the deaths of lesser Presidents such as Zachary Taylor and Warren Harding have triggered conspiracy-bent historians to call for their bodies to be exhumed to ferret out foul play, it should come as no surprise that the assassination of Abraham Lincoln—as well as that of John Kennedy—should spawn a host of historical disbelievers in the findings on their deaths. It is not easy to accept that the murder of a President is only the handiwork of one man.

I do not claim the credentials of expertise in the shooting of Lincoln in Ford's Theater on April 15, 1865. But I should admit my prejudice against conspiracy theories. (Rumors of CIA or FBI skullduggery in the assassination of Kennedy I also greet with skepticism, just as I doubt that either President Roosevelt or Winston Churchill knew beforehand of the Japanese plans to bomb Pearl Harbor and suppressed the intelligence.) I also cannot reject the "single-bullet theory" provided by the investigator (the future Senator Arlen Spector) in the Warren Commission findings. Accordingly, it is my own opinion that highly placed officials such as Edwin Stanton should not be implicated in the murder of Lincoln.

That being said, I, like any Lincoln buff, voraciously ingest any detail about the last hours or days of Lincoln's life, and the circumstances leading to his assassination.

Some Kennedy fans delight in making comparisons between Kennedy's assassination and that of Lincoln (for example, both had a Vice President named Johnson; an aide named Lincoln was secretary to Kennedy; and an aide named Kennedy was secretary to Lincoln). Such linkage seems forced.

Yet from a writer's vantage point, the personality of the principal figure in Lincoln's murder—the actor John Wilkes Booth—is a far more interesting and colorful figure than Lee Harvey Oswald, the psychopathic loner who killed Kennedy. The warped dreams and histrionics of an actor—always in the shadow of his more accomplished brother and father—ignite a writer's fascination.

"ALL THE WORLD'S A STAGE"

For actor John Wilkes Booth, the killing of Lincoln in Ford's Theater would be the crowning culmination of his dramatic career. Finally, the world would accord him for this, the greatest role in his life—the fame that had been awarded his father Junius and his brother Edwin but denied him.

After the deed, his name would not only be on the lips of Americans from New York to San Francisco, but across the ocean in London and Paris as well—in fact, across the entire world.

Those could have been his thoughts as he drank his brandy at Taltavul's, the tavern across from Ford's Theater that night of April 14. His reverie was interrupted when a barfly on the next stool recognized him.

"You'll never be the actor your father was," said the drunk.

"When I leave the stage," replied Booth, "I will be the most famous man in America."

A BAD HAND

Just before the Civil War erupted, John Wilkes Booth, on tour with a stage repertory one afternoon in Chicago, walked by a street shop with a sign advertising a palmist and went in.

The man read Booth's hand carefully and shook his head.

"Ah, you have a bad hand," the hand-reader said. "The lines all criss-cross."

The seer continued, "It's full enough of sorrow—full of trouble—trouble in plenty, everywhere I look."

The soothsayer then recited a litany of doom.

"You'll break hearts, they'll be nothing to you. You'll die young. You'll burn under an unlucky star. You've got in your hand a thundering crowd of enemies—not one friend. You'll make a bad end. You'll have a fast life, short but a grand one."

"Now, young sir," the hand-reader warned, "I never seen a worse hand and I wish I hadn't seen it."

BEER BREAK

Of all the guards assigned to protect President Lincoln, John F. Parker was the poorest choice for security detail. A year earlier he had been arrested for drunkenness and disorderly conduct at a Washington brothel. Although the charges were eventually dropped, the fact that a President's guard was drinking at a bawdy house should have disqualified him for a sensitive security position at the Executive Mansion.

Often slack in his work habits, Parker was late in relieving Colonel William H. Crook at the Executive Mansion to take his shift on the late afternoon of April 14.

Parker did, however, inspect the President's box before ushering him in to Ford's Theater when the President arrived at eight-thirty in the middle of the first act.

Yet at about nine o'clock Parker said to Burns, the President's carriage driver, "How would you like to go for a beer?"

The two went to Taltavul's, a tavern across from Ford's Theater. At the bar, Parker couldn't help but note a handsomely groomed gentleman drinking brandy with water farther up on the rail. The face that appeared on hundreds of posters was, no doubt, vaguely familiar.

It was John Wilkes Booth, who would leave at a quarter of ten to assassinate Lincoln, leaving behind the President's guard to drink his beer.

THE DEATH DREAM

A few days before the assassination, Lincoln recounted to his wife and to his friend and aide, Ward Hill Lamon, the strange dream he had just experienced. In the vision Lincoln was in his bed upstairs at the Executive Mansion when he heard people crying. He left his bedroom and went downstairs, but the rooms were empty as he walked through.

Then he came to the East Room. There soldiers were posted in guard around a catafalque upon which rested a corpse wrapped in funeral vestments.

In the dream, Lincoln asked one of the soldiers, "Who's dead in the White House?"

"The President," was the answer. "He was killed by an assassin."

Days later the President would lie in state on a bier in that same East Room.

DRAMATIC IRONY

Lincoln enjoyed the theater, but did not want to go to Ford's Theater that night of April 14. As Lincoln left for the performance, he confided to the White House guard Colonel William H. Crook, "I cannot disappoint the people, otherwise, I would not go—I do not want to go."

Then with his sad smile, he said, "Good-bye, Crook."

This puzzled the guard because always before President Lincoln had said "Good night."

DID BOOTH SAVE LINCOLN'S LIFE?

In March 1865, a young man was switching trains in Passaic, New Jersey. He was a Harvard student coming down from Boston. While he was making his way—bag in hand—across the platform to board a train for Washington, he tripped over his bag and fell into a railway pit.

A broad-shouldered man, seeing the plight of the young passenger trapped in the path of coming trains, reached down and pulled him to safety.

The twenty-year-old looked at his rescuer's face and immediately recognized him.

"You're Edwin Booth, the actor," he said.

"Yes," was the reply. "I'm headed for Philadelphia, where I'm playing *Hamlet*."

"My father," said the student, "is a great admirer of yours. I'd like to have your autograph. My name is Robert Lincoln."

"Are you any relation to the President?" asked Booth.

"I'm his son," was the answer.

"Well, you tell your father that I'm a great admirer of his."

Weeks later, Edwin's younger brother John would kill Robert Lincoln's father.

EXIT LINE

For an actor, every great role is associated with a memorable line or two. Yet as Booth played, in his mind, the greatest performance of his life, he searched for the right words that would immortalize the moment. Booth had often portrayed Brutus, the slayer of Julius Caesar in the Shakespeare tragedy of that name.

Booth remembered Brutus's words that followed the killing of Caesar, "Tyranny is dead! Run hence, proclaim, cry out about the streets. Liberty, freedom, and enfranchisement." The line, thought Booth, was too lengthy for his moment in Lincoln's box. Anyway, "freedom" and "enfranchisement" did not fit with Booth's proslavery sentiments. The shortened version—"Tyranny is dead"—might work, but reporters who were students of Shakespeare might remember the rest of the line.

The word "tyranny" probably triggered Booth's recollection of the Virginia motto "Sic Semper Tyrannis" ("Thus always to tyrants"). Booth did not know Latin, yet the slogan of the Confederacy's capital state had been translated to him. An exit line in Latin would enhance and embalm the moment. In dramatic elocution Booth would rehearse the line—rolling the *r*'s over his tongue as he intoned, "Sic Semper Tyrannis."

FACE SAVING?

John Wilkes Booth had played a hero many times onstage. But what he dreamed of was not acting a hero but being one.

In the Civil War, such dreams of glory motivated many volunteers in both North and South to offer their services.

Booth, who reviled Lincoln and romanticized the South, could have undoubtedly received an officer's commission in the Confederate Army. Why didn't he?

It was, perhaps, not cowardice but vanity that stopped Booth from enlisting in the Confederate cause. True, his mother was opposed to his fighting. Yet possibly the main reason was that he was terrified that his distinctive and striking face—the actor's trademark—would be marred or mutilated by a bullet.

THE GENERAL IS AWOL

For the April 14 performance of *Our American Cousin* at Ford's Theater, Mrs. Lincoln had invited the victorious General Ulysses Grant to sit with the Lincolns. Grant assented but later backed out. He said he had an invitation in New York, but the real reason was that his wife, Julie Dent Grant, refused to attend any function where she had to be with Mrs. Lincoln, whom she loathed.

She had good reason. A few weeks previously, Lincoln had visited the Union Army encampment in Virginia to visit the head of the Army of the Potomac, General Grant. When Lincoln arrived at Grant's tent headquarters, he found only Grant's wife, whom he talked to briefly before the general returned.

When Mrs. Lincoln later saw Mrs. Grant, she flew into a tantrum. She always had a fit when any woman talked to her husband alone.

Afterward Mrs. Grant, not by any stretch of the imagination an enticing woman, refused ever to be in the company of Mrs. Lincoln. Her insistence might have saved her husband's life.

"HAIL TO THE CHIEF"

It was to be the last night of the performance of *Our American Cousin,* but it was a flop in advance sales. True, Henry Clay Ford, the manager of the theater, knew that the play was a stale comedy. Its performance in Washington the year before had drawn mixed reviews. But Ford figured that Washingtonians would, at least, come out to see the play's star performer, Laura Keene. After all, it was Miss Keene's farewell appearance, as the promotion circulars advertised.

Yet even the featuring of America's leading women of the stage might not overcome religious inhibitions about attending the theater on Good Friday. Nevertheless, Ford had banked on the celebratory spirit of the city following the defeat of Lee to overcome compunctions of conscience. Advance sales, however, did not justify his optimism.

On the other hand, Grover's—Washington's other theater—was having a sellout with the new colorful spectacular, *Aladdin's Lamp.*

The fears of Ford quickly dissolved when a message—relayed from Mrs. Lincoln—informed him that the President and Mrs. Lincoln would be attending along with General and Mrs. Grant. "Why," said Ford to his box office manager, "Grant is the man of the hour, the most popular figure in the nation!"

Immediately Ford dispatched his staff to work. New circulars announcing the presence of the President and General Grant were circulated. Laura Keene was now demoted to second billing. The names of the distinguished guests in the promotional fliers took precedence.

As an additional draw, Ford would publicize the presentation of a newly written song, "Honor to the Troops," to enhance the mood of victory.

Then for a final patriotic fillip Ford would have the band strike up "Hail to the Chief" when the presidential party arrived—even if in the middle of the performance.

JOYRIDE?

For Lincoln, April 14 was time to savor his triumph. On this Good Friday afternoon, spring was coming to Washington as the land emerged from the ravages of winter, spring blossoms symbolically heralded the promise of peace.

Lincoln said to his wife, "Mother, let's go for a ride." At five o'clock the driver, Francis Burns, drove them in black presidential carriage down the graded path from the Executive Mansion, turning right on Pennsylvania Avenue. With two cavalrymen trailing the carriage for security precaution, the surrey sliced through the spring air that was transforming the evening breeze into a bracing tonic. As the horses accelerated their pace, Lincoln reached out to hold his wife's hand and said, "Dear, I have never felt so happy in my life."

A somber look suddenly darkened his wife's countenance. "I remember," Mary Todd Lincoln responded, "you said the same thing just before Willie died."

The merry mood that had opened the ride melted.

THE KIDNAP TRAP

The news of Lincoln's victory in November 1860 enraged John Wilkes Booth. This ugly and unkempt upstart—bereft of any breeding or background—was now President. By the time the electoral college had confirmed the election of Lincoln, Booth had already concocted a scheme to make the death of Lincoln the deliverance of the Confederacy from defeat.

Booth contemplated kidnapping the President—on one of those occasions when Lincoln attended the theater. In the Booth scenario, Lincoln would be seized and taken by flatboat down the Potomac to Virginia and then offered as ransom for favorable terms to the Confederacy. The date was set for January 18. The day came—but as fate would have it, Lincoln did not attend Ford's Theater then.

LADY-IN-WAITING

On the afternoon of April 14 Lincoln hoped to wind up his business after the Cabinet meeting early, perhaps in time to go for a relaxing carriage ride with Mrs. Lincoln. Just as he was about to leave, a black woman pushed past the White House guards to the President's office. As his aides started to maneuver the distressed woman away from his presence, Lincoln stopped them, saying, "There is time for all who need me. Let the good woman come in."

The woman announced herself as Mrs. Bushrod and she told how she and her husband had been born slaves in Richmond. The couple, with their young ones, had escaped to Washington and her husband, Tom, had then volunteered for the Union Army service in gratitude for President Lincoln's policies. Unfortunately, however, the new soldier's salary had not been received for several months and their children were starving. In response to her plea, Lincoln told her to come back the next day and the papers would be ready for her signature.

"My good woman," said Lincoln, "perhaps you will see many a day when all the food in the home is a but a single loaf of bread. Even so—give every child a slice and send your children to school."

The woman left exultantly and told listeners, "The President treated me like I was a grand lady."

". . . THE MANNERS OF GOOD SOCIETY?"

When John Wilkes Booth learned that President Lincoln would be coming to Ford's Theater to see *Our American Cousin,* Booth began devising his assassination scheme.

The best opportunity would be when the fewest actors were on the stage, because he was planning to jump from the side of the stage to the presidential box.

In the play's rehearsal, Booth saw as his best chance that moment in the play when only two are onstage. Around ten o'clock, Booth waited in the shadows on the side as the British actress playing the haughty English widow, Mrs. Montchessington, sniffed and said, "I'm sure, Mr. Trenchard, you are not used to the manners of good society and that will excuse the impertinence of which you have been guilty."

Then Booth jumped.

As Booth fired his derringer into Lincoln's head, Mr. Trenchard was answering, "Don't know the manners of good society, eh?"

"THE MARTYR PRESIDENT"

Lincoln did not want to see the play *Our American Cousin.* He had seen it once and it was funny enough, but not so amusing to warrant seeing it a second time. He tried to get out of attending, but Mrs. Lincoln would not permit it. She had last-minute troubles of her own. General and Mrs. Grant had relayed their regrets, saying they had to attend a function in Philadelphia. The First Lady would not have her own husband be a no-show, too, when she had promised his appearance. She insisted on his attendance.

"All right," he said, in his resigned, submissive way, when he found resistance was useless, "all right, Mother, I'll go; but if I don't go down to history as the martyr President I miss my guess."

He didn't miss his guess, but his little joke became a world tragedy.

THE MINISTER'S "MISSION"

John P. Hale had been one of the few Republicans in the Senate who was an outright abolitionist. In fact, Hale had run in 1852 for President on the Free Soil ticket, whose cry was "Free Soil and Free Men." Because of his radical views, Hale had been defeated for reelection as senator from New Hampshire in 1860.

Because Hale had supported Lincoln strongly in Lincoln's 1860 presidential campaign, he was entitled to some consideration by Lincoln for a good appointment.

Two weeks before his assassination, Lincoln was called on by Hale. Hale said, "Mr. President, I have to have a mission in Europe—perhaps as minister to Spain. My daughter is in love with some actor and the only way I can break up that relationship is by taking her abroad with me."

Hale's daughter, Bessie, a spoiled and rotund woman in her late twenties, had become infatuated with John Wilkes Booth, who had been toying with her affections with hints of marriage.

MURDER MISPRINT

On April 14 the Middletown, New York, *Whig Press* journal headlined a story that President Lincoln had been assassinated. Middletown was about 250 miles north of Washington, D.C. The newspaper was wrong. President Lincoln was meeting with presidential callers while its subscribers were reading the story. This New York daily was not the only one that had promoted rumors that anticipated fact.

On the same day in St. Joseph, Minnesota, there was another published report of a presidential assassination. By the time that paper tried to correct the false story for the next day's edition, news of the actual assassination had started to come over the telegraph wires.

PICKING UP MORE THAN MAIL

If John Wilkes Booth hadn't decided to stop by Ford's Theater to pick up his mail, Lincoln might never had been killed that night of April 14.

Late on that Good Friday morning, Booth left his room at the National Hotel to go over to Ford's Theater. Mail to actors was often addressed in care of the theater in the city where the performers were temporarily residing, even if the performers had no part in the play that was currently in production.

As Booth looked over his mail, he chatted with the owner, Henry Clay Ford. At about eleven o'clock in the morning a carpenter, James Gifford, came in to see Ford.

"Sir, what do you want to see me for?" asked the handyman.

Ford replied, "I want you to take down the partition between box seven and box eight—President Lincoln and General Grant will be attending tonight and we'll need all of the box space."

That piece of intelligence triggered Booth's plan for assassination that night.

PILES OF PATAGONIA

One of Lincoln's last scheduled appointments on that fateful day of April 14 was with his old pal Ward Hill Lamon, who came to him with a petition for a friend.

Lincoln sighed when he put it on his pile of petitions for relief. He said, "You know, Ward, down in Patagonia, the bottom of Chile, they eat oysters from the sea, and then chuck the shells out the window. When the heap of shells is as big as their house, they move to another house."

Then, looking at the pile of petitions on his desk, he said, "I guess it's time for me to move."

POISON PEN

The Booth assassination plot encompassed the killings of not only Lincoln but of Secretary of State William Seward, General Ulysses Grant, and also Andrew Johnson, the Vice President.

To Booth, the Tennesseean Johnson was a traitor who had betrayed his native South by joining forces with the North. In the Booth plan, George Atzerodt was to kill the Vice President on that evening of April 14. But Atzerodt was an undependable drunk. In case Atzerodt's resolve disappeared into a bottle, Booth crafted a backup scheme to destroy the Vice President's name.

That afternoon the actor went to the Kirkwood, Johnson's hotel, in hope of calling on the Vice President. The Tennesseean was out. No matter, thought Booth, he would leave his card at the desk with an affectionate greeting: "Don't wish to disturb you at home," [signature] John Wilkes Booth.

Then after Lincoln's death the hotel keeper would recall the actor's visit and the Vice President would then be implicated in the assassination. Andrew Johnson, the former Democrat governor, was not popular with congressional Republicans and the Vice President had not improved matters by getting drunk at the inauguration ceremonies a month earlier.

Yet the poison pen card would never reach Johnson. The Vice President's aide, Colonel Browning, intercepted the card before it reached his boss. Browning, a theater buff who had once met Booth, thought the card left at the desk had been meant for him.

PRESIDENTIAL JINX

For Lincoln's oldest son, Robert, the assassination at Ford's Theater was traumatic. Robert Todd Lincoln had suffered through those long hours at his father's side waiting for his inevitable passing.

Yet the experience was to be relived. Robert Lincoln was at the Washington rail depot standing next to President Garfield when the twentieth President was shot in 1882.

Again, in 1901, he was in Buffalo at the Pan-American Exposition standing next to President William McKinley when the twenty-third President was shot.

Thereafter Robert Todd Lincoln refused even to see a President or attend a function where the President of the United States would be present.

STOPPED BY A STRAP

The presidential assassination plot by Booth included the murder of the Secretary of State, William Seward.

Seward was Lincoln's "prime minister" and an object of vilification by the South even before the name of Lincoln was propelled to national recognition.

On the night of April 14, Lewis Paine (he had his name changed from Powell) was entrusted with the slaying of Seward. Seward, at the time, was confined to his house. A week earlier, he had been severely injured in a carriage accident and lay in agony in his bed in his home across from the Executive Mansion on Pennsylvania Avenue.

Lewis Paine—armed with pistol and knife—entered the Seward home under the pretext that he was delivering medicine from a pharmacy. Over the protests of Seward's black servant, Paine tried to muscle his way into Seward's bedroom. When Seward's son, Frederick, tried to stop him, Paine discharged his pistol. When it jammed, Paine felled Frederick Seward by striking him with the butt end of his pistol.

Then Paine entered Seward's bedroom, where the Secretary of State lay swathed in bandages. Paine—now maddened by the misfire of his gun—pounced on Seward, stabbing him in the neck. But the knife hit something hard—Seward's neck brace for his injury. The blade caromed to his face, slicing it as the moaning Seward rolled himself onto the floor. By this time the uproar of both the cries and calls for help by the servants had aroused the neighbors and Paine had to flee the scene.

TELLTALE TATTOO

John Wilkes Booth lived in fear that his clean chiseled face might be someday disfigured. Yet he had no qualms about marking his wrist with a tattoo.

After Lincoln's election in November, Booth began hatching his plots. Several months before the April assassination, Booth had his wrist tattooed J.W.B.

Perhaps his reason for carving his initials was to ensure his identification in case of death. What if, in kidnapping or killing the President, Booth's face were to be mutilated or obliterated by police in a rain of bullets when he was trying to escape?

A tattoo was the answer.

". . . WALK IN THE SHADOW OF DEATH"

Lewis Paine was a handsome brute of a figure if one did not look too closely at his dead eyes and dull-witted expression. If Paine was a true believer, his belief was in Booth. Paine was a social derelict whose life had assumed some kind of purpose when he met the charismatic actor. Booth had been impressed with Paine's boasts that he killed three Union Blues—not with his rifle but with his bayonet. That Paine had later deserted the Confederate ranks did not mute his bragging.

The desertion forced the new name of Paine. He had been Lewis Powell. The choice of the Revolutionary patriot's name—Thomas Paine's—gave him something in common with Booth, who had been named for the English advocate of American independence, John Wilkes.

Booth saw in his idolater a possible instrument of Lincoln's death. Booth had scouted Lincoln's movements. At the end of every day, Lincoln would stroll over to the War Office to see Secretary of War Edwin Stanton. The bushes on the path to the department headquarters offered the perfect ambush site. On March 7, Booth charged Paine with this mission and Paine, by Booth's plan, would hide in the twilight darkness of the hedge growth.

Paine saw Lincoln approach so close by that he could have stabbed, but he couldn't make himself fire his pistol. In fact, as Paine later sheepishly described his abortive ambush to Booth, he was so near Lincoln he could hear the President talk to his aide about not slipping on the ice that covered some parts of the path.

WHO KILLED COCK-ROBIN?

The death of the vainglorious assassin of Lincoln lies shrouded in mystery. The events leading up to his death, however, are clear. Booth—with leg injured by his jump from the Lincoln box—had ridden by horseback southward to Maryland. He crossed the Potomac at Anacostia, bluffing his way past a lax bridge guard. In this southern section of Maryland—forty-five miles from the capital—the fleeing actor hoped to find Confederate sympathizers. Booth did find temporary shelter, but the sympathizers' wariness regarding the wounded fugitive made the assassin resist revealing his true identity.

By April 17, Secretary of War Stanton's appointed deputy, Captain Baker, had tracked Booth to a Maryland farm. The barn where Booth lay in agony from his worsening leg injury was set on fire. Herrold, Booth's coconspirator, surrendered.

Later, Booth—delirious from a gunshot to his head—was cornered and caught. He died in the hands of his captors.

Did Shakespearean actor Booth choose the script of *Othello,* whose leading character he often played, and kill himself? "Who can control his fate? Here is my journey's end."

Or was he killed by the man who claimed the reward by Stanton—Sergeant Cobbett? The mentally unstable Cobbett—who died later in an institution—was no punctilious follower of orders.

He might have disobeyed Baker's command not to kill Booth. On the other hand, those who subscribe to conspiracy theories think Baker, as an agent of Stanton, either shot Booth himself or was responsible for Cobbett's shooting of Booth. Those who are suspicious of Stanton's involvement think Booth was killed to shut him up.

The short-range nature of the pistol firing lends support to the theory of suicide. Since Booth was not able to leave the barn and shoot it out in a dramatic finale, self-death might have been the next best theatrical ending.

WINDOW WARNING

A short time after Lincoln was assassinated, a macabre message scratched on a hotel window in Meadville, Pennsylvania, was reported to authorities:

Abe

Lincoln

Departed this

Life Aug 13, 1864

By the effects of

Poison

It was then learned that John Wilkes Booth had stayed overnight on that date in the northwestern Pennsylvania town, where he was looking after some of his oil investments.

Colleagues
and Copperheads

Abraham Lincoln liked people, but he was no extrovert. The caricature of a professional politician is the backslapper and joiner of clubs. Lincoln was neither. (He did, however, become a member of the Odd Fellows Lodge, a group not unlike the Elk or Moose lodges.)

Lincoln was shy about pushing himself before people. Yet he enjoyed the company of men—be they fellow lawyers or politicians. It is instructive that he was early elected as captain of his company of militia men and that he was the leader of "the gang of nine" (an activist group of young Whigs in the Illinois House). His very height invited a leadership role. Still, he was intimate with very few.

Unlike many in the ego profession of politics, Lincoln was a good listener, patient and responsive. Yet when he was on the receiving end of advice, he rarely committed himself. He kept his own counsel.

Lincoln was often melancholy. He would mask those moods by spinning jokes. He loved hearing and telling stories, but his tales did not—as it does for so many politicians—include gossip. While Lincoln was a moral man, holding himself to the strictest code in matters of sex and money, he was not judgmental of others. His innate racial and religious tolerance extended to the political realm. He could not bring himself to hate the slaveholders as many abolitionists did.

His only intolerance was for the intolerant—the bigots, the zealots, and even some of the abolitionists who honed their hate with religious fanaticism.

His comments about others were never etched in the acid of spite or malice. As frustrated as he might become, Lincoln kept a rein on his temper. Even his most acid asides were accompanied by a chuckle. There is in his criticism a resigned, weary acceptance of human foibles. His legend notwithstanding, Lincoln was no saint, but his patience with his nagging wife, sluggard generals, and backstabbing Cabinet colleagues might suggest otherwise.

The following quotations are Lincoln's comments about his contemporaries as well as a few encomiums to his heroes.

&a &a &a

EDWIN BOOTH (1833–1893) *American actor and brother of John Wilkes Booth, son of the famous actor Junius Booth*
    ☞ It was a good performance [Shylock in *The Merchant of Venice*] but I had rather a thousand times read it—if it were not for Booth's acting.*

---

*Edwin Booth, in shame of his brother's killing of Lincoln, retired from the stage. Only years later was he persuaded to return.

WILLIAM CULLEN BRYANT (1794–1878) *American Poet*
(*"Thanatopsis"*)

  ☞ It was worth the whole trip to meet him.*

SALMON P. CHASE (1808–1873) *Secretary of Treasury and Chief Justice*

  ☞ He's like the blue-bottle fly [who] will lay his eggs in every rotten spot he can find.

HENRY CLAY (1777–1852) *Whig Leader and U.S. Senator*

  ☞ I recognize his voice, speaking as it ever spoke, for the Union, the Constitution, and the freedom of mankind.

  ☞ My beau ideal of a statesman.

STEPHEN A. DOUGLAS (1813–1861) *Senator and Political Rival of Lincoln*

  ☞ He never lets the logic of principle displace the logic of success.

  ☞ They see in his round, jolly, fruitful face post offices, land offices, marshalships, and Cabinet appointments, chargeships and foreign missions, bursting and sprouting in wonderful exuberance, ready to be laid hold of by their greedy hands.

  ☞ You could not argue with him; the only thing you could do would be to stop his mouth with a corn cob.

---

*Lincoln was commenting on his trip to New York to speak at the Cooper Union in February 1860.

☞ I don't want to call him a liar, but when I come up square to him, I don't know what else to call him.

☞ A caged and toothless lion.

☞ He is a man with tens of thousands of followers—*blind* followers. It is my business to make them see.

SAMUEL F. DUPONT (1803–1865) *Union Navy Admiral*
☞ Like [General] McClellan, Dupont's got a case of the slows.

JOHN C. FREMONT (1813–1890) *California Explorer, 1856 Republican Presidential Candidate, and General*
☞ His cardinal mistake is that he isolates himself and allows nobody to see him.

☞ The damnedest scoundrel that ever lived but in the infinite mercy of Providence . . . also the damnedest fool.

ULYSSES GRANT (1822–1885) *Union Army General and later Eighteenth President*
☞ I can't spare this man—he fights.

☞ When Grant once gets possession of a place, he holds onto it as if he had inherited it.

☞ He's the quietest little fellow you ever saw. The only evidence you have that he's in any place is that he makes things *git*. Wherever he is, things move.

☞ It is the dogged pertinacity of Grant that wins.

HORACE GREELEY (1811–1872) *American Journalist and Editor*

☞ Greeley is an old shoe—leather so rotten the stitches won't hold. Why he is so rotten that nothing can be done with him—he is not truthful—the stitches all tear out.

HENRY HALLECK (1815–1872) *Union Army General*

☞ Have you a plan? If you have, prosecute without interference from me. If you have not, please inform me so that I can try to assist in the formation of one.

GENERAL JOSEPH HOOKER (1814–1879) *Union Army General*

☞ You have confidence in yourself, which is a valuable, if not an indispensable, quality. You are ambitious, which within reasonable bounds does good rather than harm.

THOMAS JEFFERSON (1744–1826) *Third President*

☞ Mr. Jefferson, the author of the Declaration of Independence, an otherwise chief actor in the Revolution, then a delegate in Congress; afterwards twice President who was, is, and perhaps will continue to be the most distinguished politician of our history.

☞ All honor to Jefferson—to the man who in the concrete pressure of a struggle for national independence by a single people—had the coolness, forecast, and capacity to introduce into a merely revolutionary document, an abstract truth applicable to all men and all times.

☞ The principles of Jefferson are the definitions and axioms of free society.

ANDREW JOHNSON (1808–1875) *Vice President and Seventeenth President*

☞ I know Andy and he's not a drunk.[*]

EMPEROR FRANZ JOSEPH *(1830–1916) Ruler of Austria-Hungary*

☞ He is a very wise man for he told us in the very beginning that he had no sympathy with rebellion anywhere.

MARY LINCOLN (1818–1882) *Lincoln's Wife*

☞ My wife is as handsome as when she was a girl and a poor nobody fell in love with her and what is more I've never fallen out.

GEORGE B. McCLELLAN (1826–1885) *Union Army General, Commander of the Army of the Potomac*

☞ He is an admirable engineer, but he seems to have a special talent for the stationary engine.

☞ I will hold McClellan's horse if he will only bring success.

☞ If at any time you feel able to—take the offensive. You are not restrained from doing so.

GEORGE GORDON MEADE (1815–1872) *Union Army General, Victor at Gettysburg*

☞ Your golden opportunity is lost. A good consummation was within your easy reach but you let it slip.

----

[*]Lincoln's comment after an inebriated Johnson delivered his rambling and often incoherent inaugural address as Vice President.

REVEREND PETROLEUM V. NASBY [DAVID LOCKE]
(1833–1888) *American Humorist*
☞ For the genius to write these things I would gladly give up this office.

JAMES K. POLK (1785–1849) *Eleventh President*
☞ I more than suspect that he is deeply conscious of being in the wrong—that he feels the blood of this [Mexican] war.

☞ A bewildered, confused, and miserably perplexed man.

PHILIP SHERIDAN (1813–1854) *Union General*
☞ He is one of those long-armed fellows with short legs that can scratch his shins without having to stoop over to do so.

☞ A little chap with a round head, red face, legs longer than his body, and not enough neck to hang him by.

WILLIAM T. SHERMAN (1820–1891) *Union Army General*
☞ Many, many thanks for your Christmas gift, the capture of Savannah.

☞ The most remarkable feature in the military operations of the year [1864] is General Sherman's attempted march of 300 miles directly through the insurgent region.

EDWIN M. STANTON (1812–1883) *Secretary of War*
☞ Stanton reminds me of an old Methodist preacher out West who became so energetic in the pulpit that his parishioners talked of putting rocks in his pockets to hold him down.

☞ Stanton's the rock upon which are beating the waves of this conflict. . . . I do not see how he survives, why he is not crushed and torn to pieces. Without him I shall be destroyed.

☞ It would require a surgical operation to get a joke into his head.

☞ You have been a good friend and a faithful public servant and it is not for you to say how long the country needs you.*

☞ If Stanton said I was a damned fool, then I must be one for he is nearly always right and generally means what he says.

ALEXANDER H. STEPHENS (1812–1883) *Southern Statesman, Vice President of the Confederacy*

☞ I just take up my pen to say that Mr. Stephens of Georgia, a little pale-faced consumptive man . . . has just concluded the very best speech of an hour's length I have ever heard. My old, withered dry eyes are full of tears.†

☞ You think slavery is right and ought to be extended while we think it is wrong and ought to be restricted. That is the only substantial difference between us.

---

*Lincoln was asking Stanton not to resign as Secretary of War.
†Lincoln was praising his fellow Whig's denunciation in the House of Representatives of Polk's Mexican War involvement.

HARRIET BEECHER STOWE (1809–1891) *American Author of* Uncle Tom's Cabin

☞ So you're the little woman who wrote the book that made this great war.

CHARLES SUMNER (1811–1874) *Radical Republican Senator*

☞ Sumner is my idea of a bishop.

ZACHARY TAYLOR (1784–1850) *Mexican War General and Twelfth President*

☞ What will strongly impress a close observer was his unostentatious, self-sacrificing, long-enduring devotion to duty. He indulged in no recreations, he visited no place seeking applause; but quietly, as the earth in its orbit, he was always at his post.

☞ General Taylor's battles were not all that distinguished by brilliant military maneuvers; but in all he seems to have conquered by the exercise of a sober and steady judgment coupled with a dogged incapacity to understand that defeat was possible.

GEORGE WASHINGTON (1732–1799) *General and First President*

☞ Washington is the mightiest name on earth—long since the mightiest in the cause of civil liberty—still mightiest in moral reform.

Gettysburg Gems

Carl Sandburg called the Gettysburg Address the "great American poem." It is the most memorized speech in the world. That is partly because of the brevity which rendered the address not only more beautiful but more universal. The compact 210-word address allowed hundreds of newspapers to print it and later generations of countless schoolchildren to recite it.

But it would take an assassin's bullet, the victory at Appomattox Courthouse, and the freeing of slaves in thousands of households across America to enshrine the name of Lincoln and make his words eternal.

Yet if Lincoln had yielded to the tearful plea of his wife, he would never have left his stricken son's bedside to deliver the address. Lincoln was not the featured speaker at Gettysburg—that role belonged to Edward Everett, America's most celebrated orator.

Actually, Lincoln's acceptance of the invitation surprised his Gettysburg hosts, since they thought that the President never left Washington except to visit troops. His acceptance required that they ask the President of the United States to say a few words, which they expected to be a brief salutation from the office of the President.

Lincoln, however, would seize the occasion to express the unique idea of America. Democracy, to Lincoln, was an experimental institution whose permanence was being sorely tested and tried by the war in process. Lincoln would charge the citizenry of the Republic with the mission to carry on "the cause" the fallen soldiers had fought for—the preservation of the Union. For if the war was lost, and the Union would be dissolved, democracy and its ideals of equality would be destroyed with it.

Lincoln would never have called himself an orator. He had honed his speaking style by speaking plainly to country juries. But if his delivery at Gettysburg was crisp and without flourish, his diction would impart the Elizabethan majesty of the King James Bible and Shakespeare's tragedies.

Never an elegant man, the lanky and awkward President was a contrast to the stately New England orator who preceded him. In addition to his presence, Everett's delivery had all the rehearsed gestures and ornamental elegance that the former chairman of the department of rhetoric at Harvard could be expected to manifest. Everett, who was the foremost scholar of the classical Greek elegiac expression had polished his platform style to silver perfection in hundreds of speaking appearances around the country.

After Everett's two-hour address, Lincoln was introduced by the stentorian shout of Ward Hill Lamon, the grand marshal of the event: *"The President of the United States."* Lincoln removed his shawl, took off the stovepipe hat in which he carried his speech, and then put on his steel spectacles. Yet Lincoln never looked down at the speech in his hands as he spoke to the crowd of over twenty thousand.

His high tenor drawl and flat midwestern accent were closer to the style of Midwesterner Harry Truman than the Canadian actor Raymond Massey, who portrayed him on film. Unlike the thousands who have recited his words with the enunciation of the self-conscious, Lincoln let the nobility of his words stand for themselves without theatrical adornment. Yet when Lincoln came to "the last full measure of devotion," his voice did break and the concluding words carried the same emotional pitch.

The general silence at the end of the address made Lincoln think he had failed. Yet on the sunny brisk autumn day in Pennsylvania Lincoln etched not only the creed of democracy but a masterpiece of English literature.

&a &a &a

"ALMIGHTY" AD-LIB

Lincoln never looked down at the text of the address which he held in his hand as he spoke to his audience at Gettysburg. Yet his words followed exactly the course of the drafted remarks—except for one phrase.

When Lincoln came to the words ". . . that we here highly resolve that this nation," his voice had moved into full emotional fervor. Then he extemporized ". . . shall, *under God*, have a new birth of freedom."

In the corrected text Lincoln sent out afterwards to Edward

Everett, the featured speaker of the event, he smoothed out his grammatical lapse to read that ". . . this nation under God shall have . . ."

BACK OF AN ENVELOPE?

Did Lincoln jot down on the back of an envelope notes on his Gettysburg Address? Yes.

But he had already painstakingly drafted six drafts of his address at his Executive Mansion office.

His jottings along the train ride to Gettysburg seem to have been a mnemonic device to reinforce the key words in his address. Many speakers use this note system to commit to memory an address that has already been prepared.

BANJO, BOOZE AND BAWDINESS

The train trip to the Gettysburg Cemetery rites, if long, saw few dreary faces. For security reasons, the railroad route to Gettysburg was three sides of a square—east to Baltimore, north to Hanover, Pennsylvania, west to Gettysburg. Yet the train ride was enlivened by the boisterous spirits of Ward Hill Lamon.

Lamon, an old Illinois pal of the President, officially held the office of the U.S. marshal for the District of Columbia. Unofficially, he served as a resident court jester at the White House. The banjo-strumming Lamon had a repertoire of bawdy songs and stories. While Lamon served as host, the whiskey flowed generously as he led them in singing some of his ribald ditties.

The merriment deflected attention away from President Lincoln, who reviewed correspondence and read newspapers while intermittently going over his remarks for the next day.

DEAD WRONG

The most powerful Republican of central Pennsylvania—as well as the biggest taxpayer on the Gettysburg tax rolls—was Thaddeus Stevens. Although Congressman Stevens lived in Lancaster, he once practiced law in Gettysburg and in the course acquired much property in this small town.

Stevens, however, did not attend the battlefield ceremonies at Gettysburg. Stevens had contempt for Lincoln and thought he was a sure loser in the presidential election the next year.

When Stevens was asked whether he was joining the delegation leaving Washington by train for Gettysburg, Stevens sneered, "Let the dead bury the dead!"

"DISHWATERY" DRIVEL?

It is an exaggeration bordering on falsehood to say that the Gettysburg Address—at least according to contemporary observers—was a failure. True, the Democrat-leaning Chicago *Times* called it "dishwatery, inane," and a London correspondent opined that the "ceremony was rendered ludicrous by some of the sallies of that poor President Lincoln." The Republican-leaning Chicago *Tribune,* however, said, "The dedicatory remarks by President Lincoln will live among the annals of man."

There were other discerning voices. Everett, the featured orator who had taught rhetoric at Harvard, congratulated Lincoln for achieving in two minutes what he had tried to do in two hours. John Alcott, a literary critic, found the speech sublime. Lincoln's hometown paper said it best: "It is a model that will bear re-reading."

Certainly the majority of the listeners who expressed their feelings said they were moved. Lincoln himself, however, thought he had failed. Using a country plowing term, he told his secretary of state, "It didn't scour." And Seward concurred.

"FATHER ABRAHAM"

Lincoln enjoyed the affectionate nickname of "Father Abraham" that had been popularized by Union soldiers. On the night before Lincoln spoke in Gettysburg, a group of well-wishers serenaded him outside the house he was staying in with the hymn "We Are Coming, Father Abraham."

The address he was to give the next day had an allusion to the biblical Abraham who had a son "conceived in bondage." (That referred to the fact that the child's mother, Hagar, was a maidservant. Abraham was married to the barren Sarah; later they had Isaac, who was "conceived in freedom.")

That same line ("brought forth a new nation conceived in liberty . . . ") contains another biblical note of nativity. From the New Testament, "brought forth" are the words to describe Mary's birth of Jesus.

Lincoln kept the King James version of the Bible with him, and knew it intimately. To Lincoln the language of the Bible imparted majesty to his words.

"FOUR SCORE AND SEVEN . . . "

One cannot imagine the Gettysburg Address beginning with "eighty-seven years" ago. The decision to use the archaic and biblical term was deliberate. Eleven years earlier, Lincoln had delivered a eulogy of the Whig leader Henry Clay.

At the time the Declaration of Independence was seventy-six

years old. In the address, Lincoln pondered publicly whether democracy could survive longer than the traditional biblical span for man's longevity—which was "three score years and ten." By such biblical usage Lincoln meant to underscore the fragility of the democratic idea.

GETTYSBURG "GETHSEMANE"

Lincoln never formally joined a church. He did begin attending the Presbyterian church in Springfield after his son Edward died. The church's pastor, Robert Smith, had befriended and consoled the bereft parents. Lincoln, who was a student of the Bible and the teachings of Jesus, did not, however, embrace the theology of salvation.

Yet when he saw the thousands of graves at Gettysburg, he had a spiritual awakening. As Lincoln later said: "When I left Springfield I asked people to pray for me. I was not a Christian. When I buried my son, the severest trial of my life in 1862, I was not a Christian. But when I went to Gettysburg and saw the graves of thousands of soldiers, I then and there consecrated myself to Christ."

"GOVERNMENT OF THE PEOPLE . . . "

William Herndon was Lincoln's fun-loving junior law partner. In 1854, Herndon visited Boston on a trip that combined business with pleasure. While there he went to Faneuil Hall to hear one of the country's most eloquent preachers, Theodore Parker.

Parker, a prominent abolitionist, gave to the packed hall a rousing sermon. In it, the clergyman defined democracy in a way that caught Herndon's attention.

Free government, Parker had preached, is "government *over* all the people, *by* all the people, *for* all the people."

Herndon recorded the words in a note to Lincoln.

Nine years later, Lincoln would adapt the line: "that government of the people, by the people, and for the people shall not perish from the earth."

GRAVE DIGGERS

But for a lack of gravediggers, the Gettysburg Address would have never happened. The field after the Union victory was strewn with corpses—ten thousand bodies of Union Army soldiers—not to mention the slain in the Confederate ranks. Too few were available to tote the bodies to the station to be sent by rail back for burial to states such as Ohio, Massachusetts, and New York. Some Gettysburgers did volunteer for the grisly task but in a little town with a population hardly more than two thousand it was impossible. To bury all the bodies in the confines of Gettysburg was harder still. Even if space could be found in the cemeteries of Gettysburg, who would dig all those graves?

The only solution was to have the federal government establish a new national cemetery in Gettysburg. In that case the manpower resources of the federal government might be immediately mobilized.

A quickly formed citizens' committee urged such action. The result was the purchase and setting aside of land in the battlefield for the cemetery. The dedication of seventeen acres for such a memorial necessitated a public ceremony. Thus did the planning for the Gettysburg rites begin.

INTESTINAL FORTITUDE?

One stipulation that celebrated orator Edward Everett demanded—before he agreed to accept the Gettysburg invitation to deliver the memorial address—was a "convenience shed" placed strategically behind the speaker's platform. Everett had long suffered a complaint of the bowels and required an outhouse readily accessible both before and after he delivered his two-hour address.

LAST-MINUTE "INVITE"

In August 1863 when the plans were being made for the new cemetery's dedication rites, there was no thought of inviting Lincoln to speak. Hopes centered on the acceptance of Edward Everett of Massachusetts, who was then generally regarded as the nation's most celebrated orator.

The date for the rites—originally planned for mid-September—was not scheduled two months later. November 19 was the earliest time Everett would agree to come because of the intense preparation he said it entailed.

In late October when the committee began to send out invitations to dignitaries, they realized they could not send invitations to congressmen without asking the President. But if the President did accept, it would be an egregious violation of protocol not to allow him to speak.

The committee had mixed feelings about Lincoln speaking. The President was a partisan figure and not a popular one to many sections of the public. Furthermore, some argued that the remarks by a folksy President—known for joke-telling—might diminish the reverence of the occasion. Andrew Curtin, the Republican governor of Pennsylvania, who was a political ally of the President, was asked to suggest tactfully to Lincoln that his remarks be brief as well as solemn.

NO APPLAUSE

Edward Everett received sustained applause at the conclusion of his two-hour rhetorical effort. Lincoln, after his two-minute talk, received just about none. Lincoln himself, along with Secretary of State William Seward, thought the speech a failure.

Yet a closer study of the events may solve the mystery. The twenty thousand listeners, after hearing Everett speak for two hours, were still stretching themselves and readying themselves to hear the President, when all of a sudden the speech was over. They were stunned by the quick conclusion.

Lincoln, unlike Everett, avoided the rhetorical flourish and gesture. His delivery was mostly matter-of-fact and his tempo not as deliberate as the stately cadence of Everett.

Finally, the content of Lincoln's address was more that of a prayer than a public oration. Still, the lack of applause caused some superficial observers to miss the transcendent beauty of Lincoln's words.

NO SNAPSHOT?

No photograph exists of President Lincoln delivering the Gettysburg Address. One photographer had been given the assignment. He set up his tripod about thirty feet away from the platform. Yet as he peered through his camera, he did not like the angle. So he moved his equipment and set up for another shot. Again he sighted up the subject. Still he saw a shadow across the President's face. So he once again moved his gear. Just as he had it about fixed, the

President finished. The photographer, like others in the audience, had not expected the President's remarks to be so brief.

"NOT HAVE DIED IN VAIN"

Abraham Lincoln's most reread book in his youth was Mason Weems's inspirational biography, the *Life of George Washington*. Lincoln, whose schooling was sparse, had access to few books. Those he could borrow, he did. One was the Weems book on Washington. His well-thumbed copy was destroyed when a torrential downpour seeped through the logs to soak the book.

Lincoln then had to buy the ruined edition by clearing some fields belonging to the book's owner.

Yet one page of the Washington biography which had come out of its binding was the least marred—the last page, which had been the most sheltered from the elements. It featured a woodcut of General Washington standing by the graves at Valley Forge—with the caption "That these shall not have died in vain."

The young fourteen-year-old laid out that last page which had separated from the book—which he now owned. That line would be etched in his memory and would inspire his words at Gettysburg.

"PERISH FROM THE EARTH"

The speeches and writings of Lincoln often reflect Elizabethan English—found in Shakespeare and the King James version of the Bible. Lincoln was familiar with both and his favorite biblical books were Psalms and Proverbs.

One Proverb (29:18)—"Where there is no vision, the people perish"—held particular meaning for Lincoln.

For Lincoln, the "vision" of America was the Declaration of

Independence. If the nation ever lost that ideal of freedom, it would die.

So in the Gettysburg Address Lincoln said that "government of the people, by the people, and for the people will not perish from the earth."

"PLEASE DON'T GO TO GETTYSBURG, ABE!"

Abraham Lincoln almost didn't go to Gettysburg. On the morning he was about to leave for the train depot in Washington, his wife threw a tantrum. Their son Tad had a hundred-degree fever. They had already lost two sons—Edward in 1850, who died at age four, and then Willie in 1862 had died of typhoid fever.

"Abraham," Mary wailed, "if you go to Gettysburg, I know Tad will die."

Lincoln tried to assuage his distraught wife, who begged him not to leave the White House.

With a heavy heart, Lincoln did depart. That night, after he had arrived in Gettysburg, he learned by telegram that Tad's fever had broken. Lincoln could then retire for bed.

If his son had died, would Lincoln have cut short his stay to return to Washington? If so, then America's greatest speech would never have been uttered.

"PRESIDENT" EVERETT

Edward Everett, the featured orator at Gettysburg, had been president of Harvard. Some still called him "President Everett"—instead of Congressman Everett, Governor Everett, or Minister Everett—for the silver-haired rhetorician had not only been president of Harvard University, he also had been congressman and governor. He even had served as Secretary of State. Later he held the premier diplomatic post as minister to the Court of St. James in London. Then in 1860 Everett had been a candidate for Vice President on the Constitution party ticket with John Bell of Kentucky.

Everett, who once had headed the chair of rhetoric at Harvard, was the drawing card for the twenty thousand who had flocked to the town of Gettysburg. His stately elegance of phrase made him the nation's most celebrated orator and he commanded fees that brought him close to $15,000 a year—at least $425,000 in today's market. His most famous oration was an address on President George Washington.

To many Americans, Everett was not only the most qualified man in the country to be President, he also looked and talked like a President.

THE "PROPOSITION"

Lincoln used terms of geometry in his Gettysburg Address. He saw freedom not as an axiom, as Jefferson did, but as a "proposition" to be proved. Jefferson had written in the declaration that equality was a "self-evident" truth.

Lincoln, however, did not see democracy as an automatic, self-perpetuating institution. The Civil War, to Lincoln, was a severe test of the democratic way of life. Lincoln thought it was an open question whether it could "long endure." The language of geometry would be furthered with the phrase "we here highly resolve."

Lincoln showed the draft of the Gettysburg Address to his secretary of state and most loyal cabinet minister, William Seward, who objected to the language "dedicated to the proposition," saying *proposition* was an inelegant word, not suitable to the majesty of the occasion. Lincoln declined the advice.

WON'T TALK ABOUT GETTYSBURG

In 1863, the Fourth of July celebration in Washington extended to the fifth. News of the Union Army victory at Gettysburg triggered a celebration in the capital city, which was sixty-five miles south of the Pennsylvania town.

A torchlight parade came to serenade the White House. Cries were heard for the President to appear and deliver some remarks.

Finally, Lincoln showed himself and said: "What is it eighty odd years that our nation . . . for the first time in history declared all men created equal. That is a glorious theme, an occasion for a speech. But I am not prepared tonight to do justice to that theme."

Abe's Anecdotes

Abraham Lincoln was a complex man, but no student can begin to fathom his personality unless he recognizes Lincoln's compulsion to tell stories. A Republican ally came to the President one day to seek an answer on a policy matter. Lincoln responded by saying, "That reminds me of a story . . . "

His political friend interrupted, "With all due respect, I didn't come to hear a funny story, Mr. President."

Lincoln's face turned sad. "I think if I couldn't tell stories, I'd die."

Lincoln—like some other great leaders such as Winston Churchill—was a manic-depressive. It was a fit of melancholy that broke up the engagement to Mary Todd the first time. Storytelling was his release for his moods.

The result was that Lincoln became a master at spinning funny stories. In a country where storytelling has been a staple for political talks ever since Benjamin Franklin, Lincoln is our greatest political raconteur.

In his gift for mimicry, his mobility of expression, and his phenomenal memory, Lincoln had all the endowments to make people laugh. No one in this century—be it an Alben Barkley, a Sam Ervin, or an Everett Dirksen—could rival Lincoln for convulsing an audience on the political stump.

It is not fair to judge the humor of Lincoln by what you read on the printed page. Those who heard Lincoln attested to his superb timing and innate flair for accent. He could imitate the dialect of stuffy Englishmen, a back-country rube, and, yes, a downtrodden old black. (It was not politically incorrect in those days.)

Yet Lincoln's humor, unlike that of a Lyndon Johnson or a Bob Dole, was never snide—even if he did enjoy puncturing the pretentious and deflating the pompous. Neither did he have the English humor of a Churchill or a Disraeli, with their parliamentary quips or drawing-room wit. His limited education did not allow him to play off an allusion to the classics. Lincoln was intimate with the Bible and Shakespeare, but that knowledge did not trigger the comic within him.

Rather, his storytelling was that of the parable. Like Benjamin Franklin's, his stories had a point. (*Aesop's Fables* was a frequent source of animal parables.) Franklin surpassed Lincoln in his knack for the comic maxim, but in the funny anecdote no one was Lincoln's peer.

Lincoln was the first to admit that he did not invent most of his comic stories—he was a reteller. His retentive memory stored every story he ever heard and then he adapted it. His eye for comic detail and his ear for mimicry could turn a humdrum incident into a howler.

Lincoln's sobriquet may have been "Honest Abe," but literal truth did not inhibit his storytelling. Not all those funny things happened to his neighbors and acquaintances in backwoods Illinois.

He would hear a story and tell it as if he were an eyewitness or as if it happened to someone he knew in Illinois.

Yet if there is such a thing as poetic license, there is also humor license. Good stories that illustrate a basic truth are not expected to have a notary public to affirm their veracity. President Reagan understood that—and so, for that matter, did Jesus Christ. The stories of the Prodigal Son and Good Samaritan were not historical accounts. In the tradition of his rabbinical teachings, Jesus preferred the anecdote to theological abstraction.

In collecting Lincoln anecdotes, I often found that his stories are recorded in slightly different versions by listeners or that his quips were altered to fit different audiences. For example, his reply to a Delaware delegation that the weight of their delegation would tip over the state was also told about New Jersey.

Even more than tales that poked fun at others, Lincoln enjoyed anecdotes that ridiculed himself. No famous political personality ever told more stories that mocked his looks or his humble origins.

Lincoln's stories often bordered on the barnyard, but never the bedroom. Women were not, for him, sexual objects. He would, though, take delight in putting down snobby, preening women as well as men. (He did not, however, apply such humor to "Mother," his socially ambitious wife.)

If Lincoln's quotations and longer speech excerpts offer better insights into his political views, his anecdotes more colorfully reveal his personality as well as his democratic philosophy.

&ea; &ea; &ea;

A COUNT-ABILITY

A Viennese nobleman calling on Lincoln to ask for a colonel's commission introduced himself as Count Von Schlaf. For his military qualifications, the German noble stressed his family honor and ancestry—repeatedly reminding the President that he held the noble title of count.

Taking his application, Lincoln patted the man on the shoulder sympathetically and said, "Never mind, don't you worry, you shall be treated with just as much consideration. I will see to it that your bearing a title shan't 'count' against you."

"ALL BARK AND NO BITE"

The *Trent* Affair almost caused Britain to declare war against the United States. The threat of conflict arose when a Union ship removed Confederate envoys to Britain and France from the English ship *Trent*. Escalating protests by Prime Minister Palmerston to Secretary of State Seward were handed to Lincoln. The President responded:

"I am reminded of two townspeople in New Salem whose properties had a fence that divided their backyards. Each had a hound who fiercely barked at each other from their respective sides of the fence. They ran aside the fence roaring mayhem at their canine foe—until they found a hole in the fence and then each ran for cover."

ALL BRASS, NO MASS

Congressman Samuel Shellabarger from Ohio asked Lincoln to appoint a son of a close friend to be a lieutenant in a job in the War Department. Such a staff assignment with the top brass in Washington meant no risk of battlefield death or injury.

Lincoln said, "Sam, when I started to practice law, there was a lady in New Salem who laundered shirts. A friend of mine gave her a shirt to launder. When he later put it on, he found that the whole shirt was starched all over instead of just stiff in the collar, so he sent it back saying that he didn't want a shirt that was all collar.

"The trouble with you, Shellabarger," summed up Lincoln, "is that you want an army with all staff and no soldiers."

ALMIGHTY AND ABE

At a White House reception where the guests were ushered past the President and not allowed to come too close, an old man, disappointed at not having shaken hands with the President, waved his hat and called out, "Mr. President, I'm from up in New York State where we believe that God Almighty and Abraham Lincoln are going to save this country."

Hearing this remark, Lincoln smiled and nodded. "My friend," he said, "you're half right."

"ASS-ININE"

One day a politician whose ambition outran his ability pressed his demand to be given a general's commission. Lincoln responded by recounting the story of the king who wanted the weather foretold. Finally he found, to his surprise, a stable boy who could do it.

Each day, upon the king's request, the lad would leave the palace for a time and then come back after a short while. Being curious, the king decided to have the boy followed. He learned that the boy went to a stable and asked a donkey if the weather was to be fair. If it was, the donkey's ears would go forward. If not, they would point backwards. The king, upon this discovery, made the donkey prime minister.

"But the problem was," guffawed Lincoln, slapping his hand on his knee, "that the first thing you knew, every jackass wanted to be prime minister!"

"BACKWARDS" BARRISTER

In one of his court appearances, Lincoln's legal adversary was an urbane Easterner who in addition to affecting some British mannerisms in voice had his clothes shipped from London by his English tailor. The Springfield trial took place on a sweltering summer day. Both lawyers stripped to their shirtsleeves.

The shirt of the opposing counsel had buttons down the back—which was the latest British fashion. The reverse buttoning drew stares from the rural jury.

Though the weight of the law seemed against his client, Lincoln swung the jury to his side with this sally:

"Counsel has pretended knowledge of the law," said Lincoln, "but just as he has his shirt on backwards, he has his law backwards."

BALANCING ACT

In 1864, when Lincoln's Secretary of Treasury, Salmon Chase, in a fit of rage, submitted his resignation, Lincoln asked him to reconsider. Then Secretary of State Seward—angry that his rival might not withdraw his offer—tendered his resignation, too.

Lincoln refused to accept either resignation, saying, "It's like when I was carrying back a pumpkin to home, I always needed two to keep balance. You both have to stay—you are my two pumpkins."

BIG BODYGUARD?

When General McClellan's army was positioned in western Maryland, Lincoln visited the army. One morning Lincoln took an old Illinois friend with him to look at the troops.

They climbed a hill from where the entire army of men could be seen. The President waved his hand in a gesture of half-despair and said, "What do you see?"

"Why, Mr. Lincoln," replied his companion, "isn't that the Army of the Potomac?"

Lincoln said, "No, it is General McClellan's bodyguard!"

BIG HEAD

Some weeks after the 1860 election, a banker friend of Lincoln's saw Senator Salmon Chase of Ohio emerging from Lincoln's law office.

The old friend said to Lincoln, "You don't want to put Chase in your Cabinet."

"Why's that?" replied Lincoln.

"Because," he answered, "Chase thinks he's a great deal bigger than you are."

"Well," asked Lincoln, "do you know of any other men who think they are bigger than I am?"

"I don't know that I do," the man replied, "but why do you ask?"

"Because," answered Lincoln, "I want to put them all in my Cabinet."

BIRTHRIGHT

In 1858, when Abraham Lincoln was campaigning on his unsuccessful bid for the Illinois Senate seat, he received the endorsement of the Know-Nothings, who believed only native-born Americans should have voting rights. Declining their endorsement, Lincoln said in defense of immigrants, "Who are the native Americans? Do they not wear the breechcloth and carry the tomahawk? We pushed them from their homes, and now turn upon others not fortunate enough to come over as early as our forefathers. Gentlemen, your party is wrong in principle.

"You know, gentlemen," continued Lincoln, "I once had an Irishman named Patrick cultivating my garden. One morning I went out to see how he was getting along. [Here Lincoln assumed an Irish brogue.] 'Mr. Lincoln, what do yez think of these Know-Nothings?' he asked. I explained what they were trying to do, and asked Pat why he had not been born in America. 'Faith,' he replied, 'I wanted to but my mother would not let me.'"

BLACK IS BEAUTIFUL

When the newly formed black regiments distinguished themselves in the siege of Petersburg, Virginia, in 1864, Lincoln said it reminded him of Chicago friends of his who took their old black servant to see *Othello*. The world-famous Shakespearean actor Edmund Forrest was playing the swarthy Moor in black paint. At the end of the play, the servant's host and employer asked his old retainer what he thought of the actors.

The servant answered, "Well, laying aside all prejudice and any partiality I might have, damned if I don't think that nigger outshined them all."

"BLOOD, SWEAT, AND JEERS"

In 1848 the Whigs nominated for President General Zachary Taylor, the hero of the Mexican War. Since the Whigs' only previous presidential victory was gained by a general, the party turned to that formula again. The Democratic candidate was Lewis Cass. Cass was a lifelong politician from Michigan. Since Cass was up against a popular general, he tried to pad his own military credentials.

He started calling himself "General," for Cass as governor had appointed himself head of the Michigan state militia. Soon the Democratic candidate began to insert allusions to his own battle experiences.

That prompted Congressman Lincoln to deliver a speech in the House of Representatives that poked fun at Cass's inflated war record. Lincoln did so by expanding on his own experience in the Black Hawk War—where Lincoln saw about as little real action as Cass did in the Mexican War.

"Mr. Speaker, did you know I was a military hero? Yes sir, in the days of the Black Hawk War, I fought, bled, and came away. In fact, General Cass's career reminds me of my own. Cass said he broke his sword. Well if he did break it, he did not do anything else with it! Anyway I actually bent my musket in service. And I lost lots of blood—in mosquito bites. It is said that the General was picking huckleberries during the battle of the Thames River in Michigan. Well, I surpassed him in the Black Hawk War where I made charges through the thickets of wild onion fields."

BLUE BLOOD?

Colonel Richard Taylor got his nickname "Ruffled-Shirt Dick" from a retort by Lincoln. In a debate with Lincoln, the Democratic politician played populist demagogue charging that the Whig party was owned by the rich aristocrats and manufacturing lords.

While he was speaking, Lincoln sneaked up to Taylor and pulled away his jacket to reveal a burgundy vest, a ruffled shirt with diamond stud, and a long gold watch and chain.

The drably dressed Lincoln, in old suit and coarse linen shirt, pointed his finger at Taylor.

"Behold, this hard-fisted representative of the poor," he said. Putting a hand on his own heart, he added, "And me, this aristocrat—one of the silk-stockinged gentry."

Lincoln continued, "While Colonel Taylor was making his attacks against the Whigs all over the country—riding in fine carriages, wearing ruffled shirts, sporting kid gloves, adorning his suit with massive gold watch chains, and diamond cuff links and brandishing a goldheaded cane, I was a poor boy, hired on a flatboat at eight dollars a month with one pair of breeches to my back and they buckskin."

Lincoln went on to explain how buckskin, when wet, shrinks. "There was I," said Lincoln, "getting taller with my breeches getting shorter and tighter—in fact so tight around my legs that you can see"—and Lincoln lifted up one trouser—"a faint blue streak." And, summarized Lincoln, "If you want to call this proof of my blue blood aristocracy, I plead guilty to the charge."

BOOKISH TYPE

Lincoln was once paid a visit by a spiritualist who wanted the President to plug his book. Lincoln did not want to offend the caller, but, on the other hand, he hesitated to put the presidential seal of approval to such endeavors.

Pondering for a minute, Lincoln wrote, "For the type of people who like this book, it is the type of book those people will like."

BOOZE HOUND

At one of the Lincoln-Douglas debates, Senator Stephen Douglas sarcastically referred to Lincoln's lowly beginnings. He allowed that his first meeting with Lincoln had been across the counter of a general store where liquor was sold. Douglas finally ended his remarks by saying, "And Mr. Lincoln was a very good bartender too."

A roar of laughter erupted at this, but it quieted down considerably when Mr. Lincoln answered, "What Mr. Douglas has said, gentlemen, is true enough; I did keep a grocery, and I did sell cotton, candles, and cigars, and sometimes whiskey; but I remember in those days that Mr. Douglas was one of my best customers. Many a time have I stood on one side of the counter and sold whiskey to Mr. Douglas on the other side, but the difference between us now is this: I have left my side of the counter, but Mr. Douglas still sticks to his as tenaciously as ever."

BOSOM BUDDIES?

The President was alarmed by reports of Lee's army crossing into Pennsylvania, but he chuckled at one story relayed by a scout.

It seems that in Chambersburg a young woman—fervent in her fidelity to the Union—had proclaimed to advancing Confederate troops her loyalty to the Union by covering her ample bosom with a Union flag.

One Confederate cavalry officer alit from his horse and approached the defiant damsel.

"Ma'am, you can wear what you wish, but you should know some of my buddies, when they see the Yankee colors, are great at storming breastworks."

BREATHTAKING?

A client known for embellishing his tales came to see Lincoln at his law office in Springfield.

"Abe, why that new horse I just bought galloped a mile without drawing a long breath!"

"Well, tell me now," replied Lincoln dryly, "how many short breaths did he draw?"

BRIEF "BRIEF"

An old acquaintance from Illinois who was warm in manner but not so bright in mind dropped in unexpectedly to see Lincoln at the White House. He had just been elected to Congress.

"Come in here Bob, and tell me everything you know," chuckled Abe. "It won't take long."

"BROTHER, CAN YOU SPARE A DIME?"

One morning as Lincoln was striding through LaFayette Park on the way back to the Executive Mansion, he was approached by a disheveled but sturdy man in his forties.

The ragged man, not recognizing the President, said, "Sir, can you give me a dime?"

Lincoln answered, "You look able-bodied, why aren't you in the army?"

"Sir, I tried but was turned down."

Lincoln took out a card and said, "You take this card and report to the recruitment office in the Army of the Potomac."

The Lincoln note read: "Find something for him to do. If you can't do it, come back and report to me."

BUSS BUST

From the military court came this case. An army surgeon while drunk attempted to kiss a young woman. Though he failed, the officer was cited for a court-martial. Lincoln dismissed it, saying, "I don't know as I ought to interfere on behalf of a man who attempts to kiss a lady and fails in his effort."

CAPTAIN COWARDICE

A young captain was being charged with beating up an old man. At the indictment hearing in Chicago, Lincoln began to open the case thus: "This is an indictment against a soldier for assaulting an old man."

"Sir," interrupted the defendant indignantly, "I am no soldier, I am an officer!"

"I beg your pardon," said Lincoln, grinning blandly. "Then, gentlemen of the jury, this is an indictment against an *officer*, who is *no soldier*, for assaulting an old man."

"CHANCES ARE . . . "

President Lincoln pressed General George McClellan to commit his Army of the Potomac to the pursuit and then engagement of battle with General Lee's army.

McClellan wired back, "Under fortuitous circumstances I will attack."

A frustrated Lincoln turned to an aide. "'Fortuitous'? You know what that means? One day I asked my father why men have breasts and he replied, 'In the fortuitous circumstance that men would ever have a baby—then they'd have breasts to nurse them with.'"

"Well," continued Lincoln, "'fortuitous' means the chances are about nil."

CHEAP CREEP

A visiting lawyer called on Lincoln in Salem to check up on a man his client was suing.

"Abe," he asked, "is this gentlemen a man of means?"

"Well," Lincoln replied with a laugh, "I reckon he ought to be. He's about the 'meanest' man in town."

CHUTZPAH!

In 1865, a Richmond woman came to Lincoln to complain of the damage to her house. She demanded that the government give her an award of restitution and relief. Lincoln told her it was Virginia that had seceded and initiated the war. He then added, "This reminds me of the man who murdered his parents and then pleaded for mercy on the grounds that he was an orphan."

CIRCUMNAVIGATION

A governor of Indiana stormed into Lincoln's office with some demands for military commissions. When he left some time later, the Indiana politician seemed almost benign. Lincoln's aide John Hay remarked, "Well, Mr. Lincoln, you must have given him some of those jobs because the Governor looked satisfied when he left."

"No," replied Lincoln, "I gave him nothing. I handled him the way a farmer friend of mine in Illinois coped with a big log that lay in the middle of his field.

"To the inquiries of his neighbors one Sunday the farmer announced that he had got rid of the big log. 'Got rid of it!' said they. 'How did you do it? It was too big to haul out, too knotty to split, and too wet and soggy to burn; what did you do?' 'Well, now, boys,' the old tiller replied, 'if you won't divulge the secret, I'll tell you how I got rid of it; I plowed around it.'

"Now," said Lincoln, "don't tell anybody, but that's the way I got rid of the Governor—I just plowed around him, but it took me three hours to do it, and I was afraid every moment he'd see what I was at."

CLOSED DOOR

A Republican with little to recommend him other than his party loyalty came to Lincoln.

"Mr. President," he implored, "I'd like to be appointed Door Keeper of the House."

"Have you any experience in Door Keeping?" asked the President.

"No," allowed the applicant.

"Well," pressed Lincoln, "are you familiar with the theory of Door Keeping?"

"I can't say that I am," responded the job seeker.

"Perhaps, then," continued the President, "you've attended lectures on 'Door Keeping'?"

"No, I haven't."

"Maybe you've read a textbook on Door Keeping?"

"No," stammered the job hopeful.

"Wouldn't you admit then," asked Lincoln, "that you lack the right qualifications."

"Yes sir, Mr. President," replied the rejected applicant as he departed.

"COFFEE, TEA, OR ME?"

At a hotel in Chicago the story was told how one morning at breakfast Lincoln picked up his morning beverage to drink it. He shook his head and called to the waiter.

When the waiter appeared, Lincoln said, chuckling, "If this is coffee, bring me tea. If this is tea, bring me coffee."

COLD FEET?

In 1864, President Lincoln paid a visit to the military hospital in northeast Washington, D.C. One wounded lad whose legs stretched beyond his cot immediately registered a chord of sympathy with the six-foot-four Lincoln.

"Soldier, how tall are you?"

The young man replied, "Six-five."

"Tell me friend," asked Lincoln, "do you know when your feet get cold?"

A "COLONEL" OF TRUTH

A Washington woman of some social prominence sought an appointment with the President to demand that her son be commissioned a colonel.

"Mr. President," the dowager implored, "you should know that my son's grandfather fought the British at Lexington. Why, the boy's father was in the Battle of Monterey in Mexico.

"Don't you agree," she implored, "that the service of his family qualifies my son for a commission as a colonel."

"The truth is, madam," replied Lincoln, "your family has done enough for the country. It's time to give someone else a chance."

CRIME DOES PAY!

Secretary of War Edwin Stanton filled the military prisons in Washington with those who were helping the Confederates. When a relative of a prisoner complained to Lincoln of the injustice, Lincoln told his story:

A governor of a certain state was visiting the state prison and stopped to talk with a number of prisoners. They told him their story, and in every instance it was one of a wrong suffered by an innocent person . . . but he came to one inmate who said, "Governor—I did it—I was guilty—and I have to pay the price."

"I must pardon you," said the governor. "I can't have you in here corrupting all these good men."

DEAD CERTAIN

For a possible meeting in Philadelphia, the idea of a special presidential train was broached to Lincoln.

The President questioned whether such a train was necessary, and he told of the time Robert Tyler, the son of President Tyler, went to the railroad president's office at the depot in Washington to ask for a special presidential train.

When the railroad executive denied his request, Robert Tyler said, "But didn't you furnish a private presidential train at the time of President Harrison's funeral?"

"If you bring your father to me in same shape President Harrison was, you can be certain we will give you the best train in the country."

DEATH WISH

The journalist David Locke—who would later as a humorist adopt the pseudonym of Petroleum Nasby—called on President-elect Lincoln in Springfield. The name of a recently deceased Illinois politician came up in the conversation. He was a congressman whose achievements were far exceeded by the size of his ego.

"His funeral, quite surprisingly," remarked Locke, "was attended by nearly a thousand people."

"That many? If he had known that he would have had that big a funeral," said Lincoln, "he would have died years ago."

DIE HAPPY?

In 1864, Lincoln appointed Ulysses Grant, the victor of Vicksburg, to replace George McClellan. A political ally warned him, "Mr. President, you realize that if Grant succeeds in taking Richmond, he could become the Republican nominee for President."

"Well," replied Lincoln, "I feel very much like the old man who said he didn't want to die particularly but if he had to die that was precisely the disease he would like to die of."

"DISCRETION IS THE BETTER PART OF 'ODOR'"

During the Civil War, President Lincoln dismissed one member of his Cabinet. A political ally then suggested Lincoln fire the whole Cabinet. Lincoln responded that it reminded him of a farmer he knew in Illinois who was bothered by skunks raiding his chicken coop. "I shot one skunk," the farmer said, "and it raised such a stink that I let the other seven go."

"DON'T FENCE ME IN"

When Abraham Lincoln was captain of the "Bucktail" Rangers in 1832, he was as ignorant of military matters as his company was of drill and tactics. On one occasion, his troop, marching in platoon formation, was confronted by a fence. Captain Lincoln had no idea of the proper order, but his quick wit did not desert him.

"Company dismissed for two minutes," he commanded. "At the end of the time, fall in on the other side of the fence."

DRY WELL

When a visiting diplomat praised a recently published history of ancient Greece, Lincoln shook his head. "But Mr. President," his learned guest insisted, "the author of this history is a great scholar. Indeed, it may be doubted whether any man of our generation has plunged more deeply in the sacred fount of learning."

"Yes," drawled Lincoln, "or came up drier."

EMPTY-HEADED?

General McClellan's leadership of the Army of the Potomac continued to be one of Lincoln's most vexing problems. Yet if Lincoln dismissed McClellan, what general would he pick to take McClellan's place? The top command position of the nation could not long remain empty.

One day in 1862 Senator Wade from Ohio strode in the White House and stormily demanded that Lincoln immediately fire General McClellan. Lincoln answered, "Senator, who would you put in McClellan's place?"

"Anybody," snorted Wade.

"Wade," replied Lincoln, "anybody will do for you, but I must have somebody."

FABULOUS!

Lincoln was reading Aesop's *Fables* one day after chores when his cousin Denny Hanks came to look at what book he had his head in.

"Aesop's *Fables*," snorted Hanks, "why they're just nothing but lies!"

"Yes," Lincoln said with a smile, "but dang good lies."

FACE FACTS

In the Lincoln-Douglas debates, Stephen A. Douglas accused Abraham Lincoln of being two-faced.

"I leave it to you, my friends," Lincoln retorted, turning toward his audience. "If I had two faces, would I be wearing this one?"

FAIR FARMER

Congressman Lincoln found expansionist talk of 'Manifest Destiny' troubling. To one supporter of the Mexican War, Lincoln told of a farmer he knew in Illinois.

"I ain't greedy," said the farmer, "I only want what jines mine."

FAIR OR FOUL?

One story told about Lincoln involved two young men in Lincoln's grocery store who got in a quarrel. When angry words exploded into blows, Lincoln was called upon to decide which one was right. The combatant who lost angrily threatened Lincoln.

"See here, Lincoln, I'll lick you!" he shouted.

Abe, at his six-foot-four, looked down comically at the five-foot challenger. "All right," he said, "but let's fight fair. You are so small there isn't much of you for me to hit, but I am so big, you can't help hitting me. So you make a chalk mark on me that will show your size. When we fight, you must be sure to hit me inside this mark or it won't be fair."

The idea was so ridiculous that the little bully began to laugh, and the quarrel ended as a joke.

"FALL" GUY

A persistent party member appeared before President Lincoln and demanded appointment to a judgeship as reward for some campaigning he'd done in Illinois. The President, aware of the man's lack of judicial attributes, told him it was impossible. "There simply are no vacancies at the present time," Mr. Lincoln said.

The man left. But the next morning when he was walking along the Potomac he saw a drowned man pulled from the river and immediately recognized him as a federal judge. Without a moment of hesitation, he hustled himself to the White House, barged in while the President was eating breakfast, told him what he had seen, and demanded an immediate appointment to the vacancy.

Lincoln shook his head. "I'm sorry sir, but you came too late," said the President. "I have already appointed the lawyer who saw him fall in."

FAMILY VALUES

A story is told about an appearance by Lincoln in a state legislative campaign. His opponent alluded to distinguished forebears and the eminence of his family. When he finished, Lincoln rose and began, "I only know this about my ancestry, I come from a long line of married folks."

FATHER DIVINE

After Lincoln lost to Douglas in the Senate race, he was surprised to find that the attention given to the Lincoln-Douglas debates had given the relatively unknown lawyer a national identity. In fact, Lincoln's name was starting to be mentioned as a possible Republican candidate for President in 1860. Lincoln was astonished by the turn of his luck.

He told friends of an air balloon ship that appeared in the sky above some cotton pickers near New Orleans.

A wind had blown the balloonist and his craft from a fairground some miles away. As the scarlet-and-green-striped balloon began to land, all the workers fled except for one old black, too crippled to run.

When it landed, the balloonist in star-spangled trousers and a purple-and-orange-striped coat emerged from the craft only yards from the black man.

The old black man fell to his knees and stuttered, "Massa Jesus, how's your Dad!"

FINANCIAL RAT-ING

Lincoln was asked to write, to a Chicago firm, a recommendation for a lawyer he knew who had decided to open a store.

Tongue-in-cheek, Lincoln penned his letter:

I am well acquainted with Mr. Jones and know his circumstances. First of all, I understand he has a comely wife that ought to be worth $2,500 and a new baby that's $2,500 more—and that's $5,000. He also has an office in which there is a table worth $1.50 and three chairs worth say $1.00.

But you must also take in account there is in one corner a large rat hole which would bear looking into.

Respectfully,
A. Lincoln

FIRE-MEN?

In his early years of practicing law, Lincoln often had to travel across Illinois in midwinter to get to a trial. One bitter day in February, Lincoln rode into the town where court was to be held. But when he checked into the inn next to the courthouse, he found the fireplace in the sitting room surrounded by all the other lawyers in town discussing their cases.

"Cold out there, eh?" remarked one of them.

"Colder than hell," agreed Lincoln affably.

"You've been there too, Mr. Lincoln?" asked another.

"Yup," Lincoln said with a smile, "and it's just like here—all the lawyers are standing next to the fire."

FLIGHT OF THE EAGLE

As a delegation of New York bankers was ushered in to see the President, an aide whispered to him, "These gentlemen from New York have come to see about our new loan. As bankers they are obliged to hold our national securities. Their patriotism and loyalty is unquestioned, for, as the Good Book says, 'Where the treasure is, there will the heart be also.'"

Lincoln nodded knowingly. "There is another test, I recall, that might equally apply. 'Where the carcass is there will the eagles be gathered together.'"

FOR GOODNESS' SAKE

In 1856, the Republican party nominated its first candidate for President, the explorer John Fremont. Fremont would face the Democrat James Buchanan. A third candidate was former President Millard Fillmore running on the Native American ticket.

As the Republican Lincoln canvassed Illinois for support for Fremont, one voter told him, "Abe, I don't like the Democrat—I'm going to vote for Millard Fillmore. He's a Christian gentleman—Abe, now you know he's such a *good* man."

Lincoln replied, "If *goodness* is the issue, why not write in the name of the Lord—for He has about as much chance beating Buchanan as Fillmore."

FORWARD PASS

General George McClellan's reluctance to advance the Army of the Potomac toward Richmond exasperated the President.

One day someone called on Lincoln and stated he had a family problem. His sick relative was in Richmond and he asked for a pass that would take him behind the lines.

Lincoln asked, "Are you going to really use the pass?"

"Of course, Mr. President."

"Because I gave George McClellan 125,000 'passes' to Richmond and he still hasn't used them."

THE "FOUR HUNDRED"

In 1864, some radical Republicans who were dissatisfied with Lincoln made plans to assemble in Cleveland to nominate their own President.

It was feared that thousands would come to Cleveland to register their repudiation of Lincoln.

A convention was held and the group calling themselves the "Radical Republicans" nominated John Fremont as their candidate. (He had been the Republican party candidate in 1856.)

When Lincoln was informed of the convention choice by a Republican visitor, he asked his caller how many actually came to Cleveland.

"Four hundred," was the reply.

Lincoln pulled out the King James version of the Bible he kept on his desk at the Executive Mansion, opened it to the Book of Judges, and read: "And everyone that was in distress and everyone that was in debt and everyone that was disappointed gathered unto him and he became a captain over them and they were about four hundred men."

"FRIENDLY" OBJECTION

During jury selection, an opposing lawyer objected to a certain juror on the ground that the man knew Mr. Lincoln. Judge Davis overruled the objection, saying the motion was a reflection upon the honor of a lawyer.

Abraham Lincoln then tried the same tactic, asking each prospective juror if he knew the opposing lawyer. The judge scolded Lincoln for this tactic. "Now, Mr. Lincoln, you are wasting time. The mere fact that a juror knows opposing counsel does not disqualify him."

"No, Your Honor," Lincoln answered dryly, "but I am afraid some of the gentlemen may not know him, which would place me at a disadvantage."

"FULL OF SOUND AND FURY"

In the Civil War Lincoln had to put up with a continual barrage of criticism of his conduct of the war. Lincoln told one of his strident critics the tale of a backwoods traveler lost in a terrific thunderstorm. The rider floundered through the mud until his horse gave out. Then he stood alone in the middle of the road while lightning streaked and thunder roared around him. One crash seemed to shake the earth underneath, and it brought the traveler to his knees. He cried out, "O Lord, I'm not a praying man, but I'll make the prayer brief and to the point; if it's all the same to you, give us a little more light and a little less noise."

FUNEREAL PACE

Lincoln was once called out of New Salem on an important case. He hired a horse from a livery stable. The horse turned out to be a leaden-footed nag. When Lincoln returned a few days later, he took the plodding equine back to the stable. He then asked the owner, "Keep this horse for funerals?"

"No indeed," replied the outraged livery owner.

"Glad to hear it," said Lincoln, "because if you did, the corpse wouldn't get there in time for the Resurrection."

GENERAL ACCOUNTING

When General Robert E. Lee captured Harper's Ferry, President Lincoln considered it a great calamity for the Union Army. As commander in chief, he called his generals on the carpet and tried to fix responsibility for this stunning defeat.

General Henry Halleck was summoned. He said, "I was not responsible."

"Very well," said Lincoln. "I will ask General Schenk."

General Robert Schenk could throw no light upon the matter, except to say that the blame was not his.

Then General Robert Milroy was brought into the presence of the President, and he also entered a plea of not guilty.

Next it was General Hooker's turn. "Fighting Joe" Hooker emphatically denied any culpability for the setback.

Finally, President Lincoln assembled all four generals in one room and said, "Gentlemen, Harper's Ferry was surrendered, and one of you, it seems, is responsible." He paced back and forth several times, then turned and faced the generals solemnly. "But I think I know who is."

"Who, Mr. President?" the generals wanted to know. "Who?"

"General Lee is responsible!" exclaimed the President. "Why General Lee is to blame!"

GENERAL KNOWLEDGE

Lincoln liked General Sherman and called his conquest of Savannah in December 1864 "my Christmas present."

When senators pressed Lincoln as to the general's course through Georgia in the following spring, he recounted Sherman's encounter with a Georgian plantation owner.

A gray-haired gentleman sat on the veranda of his pillared mansion as Sherman rode up to get water. The owner heard Sherman referred to as a general.

"So you're a general?" he said as he offered Sherman a jug of water.

Sherman nodded.

"How many men do you have?" queried the planter.

"About a million," was Sherman's dry reply.

"Where you be headed for?" was the next question.

"I'm not sure I should answer that," said the Union Army general.

"Oh I wouldn't tell anybody," the Southerner insisted.

"But this is knowledge not to be released publicly," stated Sherman.

"Oh I wouldn't tell anybody where you're going."

"You promise?" demanded General Sherman.

"Yes, I swear on the honor of a gentleman," said the Georgian, crossing his heart.

"All right," said Sherman, "lean over and I'll whisper it in your ear."

The man bent over and then he heard Sherman's scream.

"I'm going where I goddam please!"

GENERAL NUISANCE

While recruitment for volunteers lagged, there was no shortage of politicos pressing for Lincoln to appoint them as generals. When a visitor to Lincoln reported that a son of a mutual friend of theirs in Illinois died while serving as a private, Lincoln voiced his regret.

"I'm sorry it was not a general. I could make more of them."

GEOGRAPHY LESSON

When Attorney General Edward Bates resigned, he recommended that his assistant attorney general succeed him to the Cabinet post. But the politics of geographic balance argued against it.

"Well, I'd like to," Lincoln explained, "but he's an Ohioan and I need a Southern man. And then Lincoln added, "I suppose if the

Twelve Apostles were to be chosen nowadays, the demands of geography would have to be heeded."

GINGERBREAD MAN

In his campaign for the Senate, Stephen Douglas knew that the folksy Lincoln drew an affectionate following. Trying not to make underdog Lincoln an object of sympathy, Douglas condescendingly referred to Lincoln as "a decent honest fellow."

Lincoln replied, "Not accustomed to flattery, it was all the more sweeter to me." He continued, "I was rather like that Hoosier with the gingerbread when he said he reckoned he loved it better than any other man and got less of it."

GLAD RAGS

Political pressure from the two Ohio senators forced Lincoln to give an effete rich constituent of theirs a political job. Lincoln assigned him the consulate in Peru.

The young appointee, wearing a pearl-gray waistcoat underneath a brocaded hand-tailored suit adorned with gold buttons, called on the President.

"Mr. President," said the would-be diplomat, "I can't go to South America. I've been told they have bugs that are liable to eat up one's inside."

"Well," replied Lincoln as he looked over the man's gaudy garb, "if they do, they'll leave behind a very fancy suit of clothes."

GLOBE SPOTTER

Simon Cameron was not only the Secretary of War, but Pennsylvania's most powerful politician. When Lincoln was urged to appoint a certain Pennsylvanian to a political job, he had to check with Cameron for his approval.

Cameron was not pleased that a political enemy of his was up for appointment. He strode into Lincoln's office.

"Mr. President," he said, "I won't object if you send this man abroad—way abroad." Seeing a huge globe in the presidential office, Cameron wrapped his arm around it—his forefinger touching a remote spot on the opposite side.

"That's where you can send him," said Cameron. Lincoln looked at where Cameron's finger rested. It was Russia. And that was where the secretary of war's foe was a given a diplomatic appointment.

GOD SQUAD?

During the Civil War, a delegation of Methodist clergymen called on the White House. The spokesman of the group intoned, "Mr. President, our cause will prevail, because the Lord is on our side."

"Gentlemen, the question we should always ask ourselves is: 'Are we on His side?'"

"HAIR"-BRAINED

When a report from a congressional committee on an aspect of the war was plunked down on Lincoln's desk in the White House, Lincoln fingered the pages of the huge tome and muttered his exasperated comment.

"Why can't an investigating committee show a grain of common sense? If I send a man to buy a horse for me I expect him to tell me that horse's strong points—not how many hairs he has in his tail!"

HALF-BAKED

A Chicago hotel where Lincoln was staying featured ice cream. Lincoln pretended not to know of the dessert special. When the ice cream was served after dinner, he took a spoonful and recoiled, saying, "Say, waiter, I don't want to slander this hotel, but this here pudding's half-froze!"

HATS OFF TO YOU

At a reception at the Executive Mansion, Lincoln noticed in the receiving line a woman wearing a very frilly hat. He was just about to compliment her on her millinery confection when he saw behind her another woman also in ornate chapeau.

Tactfully, the President said, "Your hats mutually excel each other."

HEAD UP HIS A--?

In 1864, Lincoln replaced George McClellan with Joe Hooker. The new head of the Army of the Potomac, like his predecessor, manifested more posture than progress.

Hooker, who tried to clothe himself in the style of a take-charge leader, soon wrote a memo to Lincoln signed, "From his headquarters in the saddle—Joe Hooker."

Lincoln replied to his staff, "Hooker seems to have his headquarters where his hindquarters ought to be."

"HEARTBREAK HOTEL"

A Southerner who was a Unionist called on the President. He was a New Orleans man who had been evicted by Louisiana authorities.

"Mr. Lincoln," he said, "when they called at my house, I asked them to show me a writ or some legal document. Then the official who was physically forcing me onto the boat leaving New Orleans explained, 'We don't have no papers because we don't want to have on record anything that's illegal or unconstitutional.'"

Lincoln told the Louisianan, "Why, that brings to mind a hotel in St. Louis that advertised that no one ever died in their establishment—that was true but during a cholera outbreak, they put patients that were dying out on the sidewalk."

HE GOT A CHARGE OUT OF THAT

On a visit to see Edwin Stanton in the War Department, Lincoln was suddenly bowled over while walking down a corridor. A major running in the opposite direction had slam-banged into the President.

The major was chagrined as he helped his commander in chief up. "Mr. President," he blurted, "ten thousand pardons."

"One is enough." Lincoln smiled. "I only wish the Army of the Potomac would charge like that."

HOG-TIED?

In 1860, as the Republican presidential nominee surveyed his prospects, Lincoln heard from his Republican managers in New York. The Democratic party in that state, he was informed, was divided between Tammany Hill Democrats, "Loco-Focos," "Barn-Burners," and Van Buren Democrats.

Lincoln said it reminded him of an indictment in Chicago that read, "He did steal, abscond and appropriate 10 boars, 10 sows, 10 shoats and 10 pigs . . . "

When the farmer heard the indictment, Lincoln added, "Why, that's the most evenly divided gang of hogs I ever heard of."

HOG-WILD

As a lawyer for the railroad, Lincoln once found a demand in a damage suit exorbitant. As he discussed a settlement with the opposing counsel, he told of a farmer he knew near New Salem, who raised a 350-pound hog. Talk of the huge hog spread and another pig farmer made a fifteen-mile trip to see the stupendous swine specimen.

The visitor was told he had to pay 25 cents. He forked over two bits and then started to walk away. "Don't you want to see the prize hog?" said the raiser.

"No," said the departing caller, "I've already seen the prize hog."

HOLD YOUR HAT!

On Inauguration Day in March 1861, a platform was erected over the steps of the eastern portico of the Capitol for the swearing-in and speech ceremonies. Suddenly the President-elect appeared. He wore a shawl and a tall silk hat. In his right hand was a cane. The cane Lincoln put under the table. He then took off his hat and pulled out his speech manuscript with his right hand. But he didn't know what to do with the hat. Senator Stephen A. Douglas, his former presidential opponent, quickly stepped forward, took the hat, and returned to his seat. "If I can't be President," he said to one of Mrs. Lincoln's cousins, "I can at least hold his hat."

HOLE-IN-ONE?

In 1864, President Lincoln, frustrated by the indecision of General McClellan, went to see him at his tent headquarters. As

Lincoln made his way through the encampment of the Army of the Potomac, he was recognized by a couple of carpenters putting up some kind of shed.

One of them called out, "Mr. President, we're making an outhouse for General McClellan!"

Then the other workman yelled, "Should we make it a one-holer or two-holer?"

"Better make it one hole," Lincoln said with a chuckle. "Why, McClellan would dither so much deciding which to use—he'd shit in his pants."

HOMEBODY?

Abraham Lincoln made many self-deprecating jokes about his homely appearance. Once while speaking to a convention of newspaper editors in Bloomington, Indiana, he said he felt out of place there because of his lack of literary credentials and he wondered whether he should have come at all. "I feel like I once did when I met a woman riding on horseback in the woods. As I stopped to let her pass, she also stopped and looked at me intently and said, 'I do believe you are the ugliest man I ever saw.'

"'Madam,' I said, 'you are probably right, but I can't help it.'

"'No,' said she, 'you can't help it, but you might stay at home.'"

HONOR "ROLE"

After an evening at the White House, Lincoln was asked, "How does it feel to be President of the United States?"

"You have heard," said Lincoln, "about the man who was tarred and feathered and ridden out of town on a rail? A man in the crowd asked him how he liked it, and his reply was, 'If it wasn't for the honor of the thing, I'd rather walk.'"

HORSE LAUGH

At a Springfield tavern, lawyer Lincoln and his friend Judge Davis exchanged stories about the worst horses they'd ever had. The two then made a wager that the next day each would bring a horse to the inn and then they would have to swap.

The following morning Judge Davis dragged by tether the sorriest excuse of an equine specimen. Davis was met by Lincoln, who was carrying a sawhorse.

Lincoln looked over the old plug and said, "This is the first time I've ever been beaten in a horse trade."

HORSE POWER

A loyal supporter came to Lincoln to warn him of his secretary of treasury's presidential ambitions. Salmon Chase, Lincoln was told, was planning to replace him as the Republican presidential nominee in 1864.

In response, Lincoln asked his political friend, "Do you know what a 'chinfly' is?"

When his friend shook his head, Lincoln explained that it was a big stinging horsefly.

"A neighbor of mine," related Lincoln, "had this lazy plow horse. One day a visiting farmer saw a chinfly alight on this sleepy horse and shooed it away.

"'Why did you do that?' said the farmer. 'That chinfly is what gets that horse moving.'

"Well," continued Lincoln, "if Chase has a presidential 'chinfly' biting him, I'm not going to knock it off. It will only make his department go."

HOT STUFF

Simon Cameron was a Pennsylvania political leader who helped swing the Keystone State's convention votes to give Lincoln the Republican nomination. Lincoln's managers promised Cameron a major Cabinet post. That turned out to be the War Department.

When President-elect Lincoln announced the appointment of Cameron as secretary of war, Cameron's bitter political rival in Pennsylvania, Congressman Thaddeus Stevens, announced, "The only thing Cameron wouldn't steal is a red hot stove."

Lincoln, hoping to placate Cameron, asked Stevens to recant.

The irascible congressman came to the Willard Hotel where Lincoln was staying before the inauguration and said, "I have been asked to retract my statement 'The only thing Cameron wouldn't steal is a red hot stove.'

"I now do—he would."

Though that was not the public statement Lincoln wanted, privately he relished telling the story.

HOW NOW, BROWN COW?

A telegram from General McClellan was rushed to the President's desk. Lincoln sliced it open, hoping it contained news of an important victory.

The cable read: "Have captured two cows. What disposition should I make of them?"

An exasperated Lincoln wired back: "Milk them."

HUFF AND PUFF

In one debate with Stephen Douglas, Lincoln poked fun at the Democrat's attempted rationalization of slavery in the Territories.

"When I was a boy," Lincoln said, "I spent considerable time along the Sangamon River. An old steamboat plied on the river, the boiler of which was so small that when they blew the whistle, there wasn't enough steam to turn the paddle wheel. When the paddle wheel went around, they couldn't blow the whistle.

"My friend Douglas," he continued, "reminds me of that old steamboat, for it is evident that when he talks he can't think, and when he thinks he can't talk."

INSIDE TRACK

Abe Lincoln did some hitchhiking in his younger days. Of course, in those days the best a hitchhiker could hope for would be a ride in a horse-drawn carriage.

One hot summer afternoon Lincoln was walking down a dusty road when a stranger came along driving a buggy. Lincoln, whose coat was slung over his shoulder, called out to the driver, "Sir, will you be so kind as to take my overcoat to town for me?"

The man in the buggy was perplexed by this request but agreed to it. "But how will you get your overcoat back again?" he asked.

"Oh, that's easy," said Lincoln, putting on his coat. "I'll stay right inside it."

IT TAKES ONE TO KNOW ONE

During one of the Lincoln-Douglas debates, a heckler yelled at Lincoln, "You're a fool!"

Lincoln turned to his taunter and dryly answered, "Well that makes two of us."

JUDICIAL ENLIGHTENMENT

In one contractual litigation, Lincoln appeared before the justice of the peace, whose learning of legal matters was minimal.

To various points in Lincoln's argument, the befuddled magistrate would answer, "I just don't know about that."

When for the fourth time the township jurist stammered, "Well, I just don't know about that," Lincoln answered:

"I *knew* Your Honor didn't know about it and that's why I just told you."

JUST DUCKY

Like most humorists, Abraham Lincoln could not resist the temptation to indulge in an occasional pun. Once when he was gazing out the window of his law office in Springfield, Illinois, he saw a plump and stately matron wearing a plumed hat and making her way gingerly across the muddy street. Suddenly she slipped and fell back on her buttocks. "Reminds me of a duck," he told Herndon, his law partner, who was standing beside him.

"How so?" asked his partner.

"Feathers on her head," said Lincoln, "and 'down' on her behind."

KILLER FOR DETAIL

Back in Illinois, lawyer Lincoln often appeared before a jurist who had a reputation as a "hanging judge."

Yet as hard as he was on criminals who violated the law, he was just as tough on lawyers who didn't follow procedure. Said Lincoln:

"He would hang a man for blowing his nose in the street but would quash the indictment if it failed to specify which hand he blew it with."

KING CHARLES'S HEAD

In February 1865, three Confederate commissioners met with President Lincoln and Secretary of State Seward in Hampton, Virginia. At the opening Lincoln laid down the ground rules. "I will not bargain with armed troops warring against the government."

"But Mr. Lincoln," argued one Confederate commissioner, "didn't King Charles I meet with the Cromwell's Roundhead troops during their Civil War?"

Lincoln turned to Seward and asked, "Secretary, you are a student of English history. Am I not right that was the conflict where King Charles lost his head!"

KNOW-IT-ALL

A dark-haired woman burst into Lincoln's office. Her eyes eerily bore into the President as she demanded, "I want to be given a hospital."

"You're a nurse?" asked Lincoln.

"No," was her reply. "I do much more than a nurse."

"You're a doctor then?" Lincoln asked.

"No, I do much more than a doctor," she explained. "I'm a clairvoyant. I can just look at a person and know what's ailing him."

"How's that?" was Lincoln's quizzical reply.

"Mr. President," she said, "I can see through you right now. I see your liver, I see your lungs. They are pink and glowing with health. You will live another twenty years."

"Ma'am," Lincoln said gently, "you know much too much for any hospital."

LINCOLN LOAN

For a long while during the Civil War, General McClellan, commander of the Army of the Potomac, did not commit his troops to battle. His frustrated commander in chief sent him a note: "My dear McClellan, If you don't want to use the Army, I should like to borrow it for a while."

LION AT LARGE

In his circuit court days, Lincoln once encountered a prissy judge.

In a trial this judge corrected Lincoln, "Counsellor, you are mispronouncing 'lien.' The 'i' is long like 'lye-en.'"

The pedantic judge again interrupted Lincoln in his explanation to the jury when Lincoln said ". . . this lien on the property," and corrected him. "It is pronounced in two syllables- 'lye'-en.'"

"Your Honor," Lincoln answered, "if my client had known there was a *lion* on his farm, he wouldn't have stayed there long enough to bring this suit."

LION TAMER

After Lincoln was inaugurated, the immediate threat was the vulnerability of Fort Sumter off the South Carolina coast. One adviser recommended to Lincoln that the Union yield Fort Sumter, Fort Pickens, and other federal government properties in the South.

Lincoln said, "There is a lesson in the fable of the lion and the woodman's daughter.

"A lion was very much in love with a woodman's daughter. The fair maid referred him to her father. The lion applied for the girl. The father replied, 'Your teeth are too long.' The lion went to a dentist and had them extracted. Returning, he asked for his bride. 'No,' said the woodman, 'your claws are too long.' Going back to the dentist, he had them drawn. Then he returned to claim his bride, and the woodsman, seeing that he was unarmed, beat out his brains."

Lincoln concluded, "May it not be so with me, if I give up all that is asked?"

"LITTLE BOY BLUE"

A fourteen-year-old boy from Kansas had left the family farm to be a drummer boy for the Union Army. Clad in his new blue uniform, the boy had sounded the drums for charge but then had fled when he experienced the bloody action that followed.

When the lad was caught, he was sent to Washington for action to be taken for his desertion. There he was taken by the officer to the Executive Mansion. Thinking he was to be shot at sunrise, the wretched youth was sobbing as he was led into the President's office.

Lincoln took one look at the miserable youth and wrote out a note to take back to his commanding officer.

When the officer opened the presidential envelope, he saw a note and authorization for a night at a hotel and train fare back to Kansas: "Hadn't we better spank this little boy and send him back to his family?"

THE "LITTLE KERNEL"

Alexander Stephens had been a fellow Whig congressman and friend of Lincoln's in the past. As Vice President of the Confederacy, he was selected to embark on a peace mission to see President Lincoln in February 1865.

On February 3, a wintry day in a boat off Fortress Monroe, Lincoln and Seward, his secretary of state, met Stephens and another Confederate commissioner. Stephens, who barely topped five feet, began divesting himself of his clothes in the warm cabin near the boiler. Off came his overcoat, his wool hat, three scarves, two vestments, and a jacket.

Lincoln looked at the diminutive Stephens and then the mass of clothes left in a pile on the cabin floor and said, "Never have I seen so much shuck with such a little nubbin."

LOCAL OPTION

Lincoln, while walking to a political meeting, saw a carriage in the distance. Although the driver was Lincoln's Democratic opponent for the legislature, he stopped to pick up Lincoln.

In the two-man debate that was held later at the meeting, Lincoln was the second to speak.

"As a poor man I don't have a carriage and my opponent kindly gave me a lift in his carriage. Now I'm here today to ask for your support for my re-election to the legislature. But if you can't vote for me, I wish you vote for my opponent who is a fine gentleman."

LOUSY AIM

As a state legislator Lincoln introduced a bill to build a road to New Salem. A Democrat in opposition fulminated that he saw in such legislation violations of the Constitution.

Lincoln replied that it reminded him of a seedy farmer he knew who never took a bath. One day he hoisted his rifle to shoot a squirrel he saw in the garden. He fired three shots and said to a neighbor watching, "Did I get him?"

"Get what?" replied the neighbor.

"That squirrel," replied the old codger.

"What squirrel?" repeated the neighbor.

"The squirrel in the garden."

"There was no squirrel," replied the onlooker. "You must have had a louse in your eye—and thought it was a squirrel as you squinted to aim."

Concluded Lincoln, "My honorable opponent sees a violation of the Constitution when it's only a speck of a varmint in his own eye."

MANLY VIRTUE?

Abraham Lincoln was a soft-hearted man who found it difficult to turn down the many requests made of a man in his position. After he signed one pardon, he told an aide, "I thank God I was not born a woman, because I never could refuse an impassioned plea."

MINIMAL MISTAKE

Lincoln was once asked if he ever admitted past errors and apologized for them.

"Yes," replied Lincoln, "I do make amends for my big mistakes but not for little ones."

"What do you mean by a little mistake?" questioned his companion.

"Well," drawled Lincoln, "I once said 'liar' when I meant to say 'lawyer'—but there was such little difference that I didn't correct it."

MILE NIGH?

Senator Ben Wade led a delegation to the White House to register their complaints. "Mr. President," Wade said, "this administration is going right to perdition. Why, it's only a mile away from Hell right now."

And Lincoln replied, "Well, Senator that's just about the distance of the White House to Capitol Hill."

MILITARY MATH

Mr. Lincoln sometimes had a very effective way of dealing with journalists who bothered him with questions. A reporter once asked him how many men the rebels had in the field.

The President replied very seriously, "Twelve hundred thousand, according to the best authority."

The astonished newsman grew pale and sputtered, "Good heavens!"

"Yes sir, twelve hundred thousand—no doubt of it. You see, all of our generals, when they get whipped, say the enemy outnumbers them from three or five to one, and I must believe them. We have four hundred thousand men in the field, and three times four make twelve. Don't you see it!"

MINORITY RULE

When President Lincoln first met with his Cabinet to present his proposed Emancipation Proclamation, he asked for a vote on the issue.

The Cabinet voted overwhelmingly against it. After all the "no" votes had been counted, Lincoln raised his right hand and said, "The ayes have it!"

MONKEY BUSINESS

Lincoln finally thought he had the man to head the Army of Potomac: the hero of Vicksburg, Ulysses Grant. Grant came to the Executive Mansion. Before assigning the command, Lincoln sought some assurances from Grant. The President had been frustrated with generals such as McClellan, Hooker, and Burnside, who kept demanding more troops but not committing them to battle.

"Grant," Lincoln said, "before I give you this commission I want to tell you this tale of the jungle monkey.

"Well—the animals," he said to Grant, "were looking for a leader. All refused. At last the monkey agreed to do it on one condition—that he have more tail. Another creature volunteered his tail and it was spliced onto the monkey's caudal appendage. The monkey admired his extended tail but still thought it should be longer. Additional tail was added but that was still not enough. The monkey wanted an even longer tail. Even then the monkey was not content. More tail was added. It was then so long the monkey had difficulty dragging it behind him. So finally they wrapped the elongated tail around him and looped it around his neck. The result," concluded Lincoln, "was that the monkey strangled in his own tail."

Grant nodded. He got the message.

MUTUAL "TRUSS"

When Lincoln assumed the presidency in 1861, many states in the South threatened secession. One Northern Democrat urged him to make peace overtures to the South. Lincoln, however, was skeptical of any reciprocal commitments the South would make in response.

He said that it reminded him of a builder who boasted of his construction skills.

The engineer bragged, "Why I could build a bridge anywhere—even to the infernal regions of Hell."

"Well," his listener said to the engineer, "I do think you could erect such a bridge but I have my doubts about the abutments on the other side."

"MY KINGDOM FOR A HORSE"

If the army was continually beset by a lack of supplies, there was no shortage of politicos demanding of Lincoln that they be commissioned generals.

One day a military aide reported to Lincoln:

"Mr. President, there was a major defeat in southern Ohio—a brigadier general was captured and so were a hundred and twenty horses."

Lincoln replied, "That's sad—I mean about the horses—I can easily replace the general but not the horses."

NAG-GING CONCERN?

The litany of excuses that General McClellan sent to Lincoln about his delay in marching toward Richmond seemed endless. Perhaps the worst was McClellan's telegram one day that the horses in his cavalry were "all sore-tongued and fatigued."

Lincoln wired back, "Will you pardon me for asking what the horses have done since the Battle of Antietam that would fatigue anything?"

NAME YOUR POISON

During the Civil War, Secretary of War Edwin Stanton delivered this confidential report to the President:

"Mr. President," intoned the bearded Stanton gravely, "I must tell you that witnesses have observed General Grant actually imbibing in his tent."

"Is that so?" drawled Lincoln. "Can you tell me what brand of whiskey he's drinking?"

"I don't understand why that is necessary," replied his confused secretary of war.

"Because," answered Lincoln, "I want to send a case of it to my other generals."

NECKTIE PARTY

As Lincoln left the White House for the train depot to embark on his Gettysburg trip, an aide tried to hurry him.

"Mr. Lincoln, we're running late." Lincoln smiled and said, "That reminds me of a horse thief back in Illinois. The cart that was carrying him to the gallows was slowed by the pressing crowds jostling to get close to the action.

"The man to be hanged yelled out to the rushing throngs. 'Now just take it easy there,' he said, 'you all know there ain't going to be any fun till I get there.'"

NO CRYBABY

Just after the Illinois legislature elected Stephen A. Douglas in 1859 to be U.S. senator, a friend of Lincoln asked him how he felt about the defeat.

"I feel like the little boy who stubbed his toe and he said 'I'm too big to cry but it hurts too bad to laugh.'"

NO DRAFT DODGER

A grizzled farmer whom Lincoln knew from his years in New Salem took his first trip to the nation's Capitol and then called on the President.

He clapped Lincoln on the shoulder and said, "Well, old hoss, how are you?"

Lincoln shook his head but smiled at the codger's reference to him, saying, "So I'm an old hoss, am I? What kind of hoss, pray?"

The old farmer answered, "An old draft horse."

"Well," replied Lincoln, "like a lot of others I'm drafted for the duration."

NO GRAVEN IMAGE

President Lincoln was once shown a painting that was perhaps ahead of its time in its nonrepresentational departure from the laws of perspective and proportion.

Asked his opinion of the canvas, Lincoln cleared his throat. "Why, the painter is a very good painter. He observes the Lord's commandments."

"What do you mean by that, sir?"

"It seems to me," Lincoln answered thoughtfully, "that he hath not made unto himself the likeness of anything that is in the heaven above, or that is in the earth beneath or that is in the waters under the earth."

NO JOKING MATTER?

Sometimes after Lincoln finished telling one of his stories in his White House office, he would tell this story about two Philadelphia Quaker ladies who were discussing the outcome of the war over tea.

"Thee knows," said one, "that Mr. Davis is a praying man."

"Yes," replied the other, "but so is Mr. Lincoln a praying man."

"That's true," said the other, "but the Lord will think that Abraham is joking."

NO PET PROJECTS

In 1863, the Union Navy had not captured or closed any major harbor in the South. When the secretary of the navy, Gideon Welles, and the naval chief of staff outlined the difficulties in the taking of the port New Orleans, Lincoln listened patiently and replied, "Gentlemen, the objectives you have insisted on following in the past have resulted in some victories—but they were easy ones.

"I am reminded of an old woman in Illinois who suspected a skunk of killing some of her chickens. Her husband sat up with a shotgun all night and in the morning brought her two dead rabbits. 'Them's two of them skunks I kilt.'

"'Them ain't skunks,' said the old woman. 'Them's my pet rabbits, you always was a fool!'

"'Well then,' returned the old man, 'if them ain't skunks I don't know a skunk when I sees it.'

"Now, Mr. Secretary," said the President, "the Navy has been hunting pet rabbits long enough—suppose you send them after some real skunks."

NO "SHRINKING VIOLETS"

Lincoln once attended a Methodist church bazaar in Washington as President. Buying a bunch of violets, he gave the lady at the booth a $20 bill. She made no attempt to make change and gushed, "Oh, thank you, Mr. President."

At this Lincoln reached down from his great height, gently touched the woman's wrist, and asked, "What do you call this?"

"Why, Mr. President, that is my wrist. What did you think it was?"

Replied Lincoln, "Well, I thought it might be your ankle, everything else is so high around here."

"OATH" OF OFFICE

Of all those who held office in Lincoln's Cabinet, none was more loyal than his secretary of state, William Seward. Yet in pressing for certain diplomatic decisions by Lincoln, Seward would often punctuate his arguments with profanity.

Once while riding Lincoln up to the Capitol, the carriage wheels got stuck in the mud and the driver unleashed a blue spate of holy curses. Lincoln got out of the carriage and asked, "Tell me, driver, what Episcopal church do you go to?"

"What makes you think I'm an Episcopalian?"

"Well, Mr. Seward goes to the Episcopal church and you talk to God just the way he does."

"OLD KENTUCKY HOME"

When it was reported that Confederacy President Davis had promulgated a death sentence for runaway slaves, a caller on Lincoln said, "It's just incredible to think that you and Jeff Davis were born in the same state."

"Well," replied Lincoln, "my home state of Kentucky is an agricultural wonder—it can produce just about anything."

OUT OF HIS HAIR?

A congressman who was always pestering Lincoln came to press another concern. The politician—bald as a cueball—launched into his complaint.

Lincoln, hoping to make it a short call, excused himself to go to his closet.

Picking out a small bottle of tonic, Lincoln came back and said, "Congressman, I have here just what you need. It'll cure baldness."

"It will?" asked the cue-ball domed legislator.

"Oh yes," reassured Lincoln, "it will make hair grow on a pumpkin. Take it," he prescribed, "and use it daily. Then come back to me in eight months."

The happy caller rushed out of the office eager to try the elixir. As soon as he left, Lincoln collapsed with laughter.

OUT OF SIGHT

As a young man Lincoln volunteered for the county militia during the Black Hawk War. The gangly twenty-two-year-old was among a group to pass inspection in front of the militia major. The officer, hardly more than five feet in stature, barked at Lincoln.

"Stand straight, soldier."

Lincoln pulled himself up.

"I said straight," yelled the martinet major. Lincoln, with all his six-foot-four height, stood ramrod straight.

"Didn't you hear me? I said straight," cried the bullying officer.

Lincoln exhaled. "If I stand taller it's goodbye, Major, for I'll never see you again."

PATIENCE OF JOB

One day an old man came to Lincoln to ask for a pardon for his son, who'd been court-martialed for dereliction of duty. "I am sorry," said the President, gently but firmly. "I can do nothing for you. Listen to this telegram I received from General Butler yesterday: 'President Lincoln, I pray you not to interfere with the courts-martial of the army. You will destroy all discipline among our soldiers.'"

The old man's face fell. When Lincoln saw his hopeless despair, Lincoln sighed and wrote out his order and then showed it to the old man:

Job Smith is not to be shot until further orders come from me.

—A. Lincoln

"Why, I thought you wrote out a pardon," said the father disconsolately. "You may order him to be shot next week."

"My old friend," said Lincoln, "I see you are not very well acquainted with me. If your son never dies until orders come from me to shoot him, he will live to be a great deal older than Methuselah."

PEEPING TOM

In 1861, Senator Stephen Douglas came to President Lincoln because his brother-in-law was in danger of losing his government patronage job. It seems he had been caught looking over the window transom on a hotel door in Washington while a visiting French actress was disrobing.

"Well, Senator, I'm not dismissing him," Lincoln informed him. "Actually I was thinking of promoting him to a . . . 'peerage.'"*

PETTIFOGGERY

Lincoln in the 1850s often represented the Illinois Central Railroad. He frequently encountered in trials an attorney whose orotund language masked a shallow knowledge of the law.

Lincoln said of one prolix lawyer, "He can compress the most words into the smallest ideas of any man I ever met."

PLATFORM PERFORMER

One of President Lincoln's most onerous duties was sifting through the mountain of job applications. It has been said that Lincoln once told about a job applicant who filled out all the blanks but was stumped when it came to explaining "Death of Father." That was a sensitive issue, since his father was a horse thief who had been hanged. Lincoln said the job-hunter chewed his pencil and then wrote, "My father was participating in a public ceremony when the platform gave way."

"POOCHIE" PIECES

A Republican senator critical of Lincoln's war leadership asked the President why the Union Army couldn't defeat Jubal Early in Virginia. Lincoln, who had just received a telegram from General

---

*Lincoln, perhaps because of his gratitude for Douglas's support of his war policies, did not fire the errant official, who also had been arrested on an assault charge. However, he wrote the man that he owed it to himself and his family to shape up.

Philip Sheridan that he had decimated Early's Confederates in a series of victories in the Shenandoah Valley, said, "Senator, General Early's army is no more!"

"In fact," continued Lincoln, "it reminds me of a farmer I knew who was threatened by a savage dog. He took a piece of dynamite powder, lit it, clapped it inside a biscuit, and tossed it to the dog that was snarling at him. Well, the dog snapped it up and swallowed it. Presently the fire touched the powder and away went the dog, his head in one place, a leg here and another there, and the different parts scattered all over the country.

"'Just pieces, but as for the dog, as a dog,'" said the farmer, 'I was never able to find him.'

"And that," summed up the President, "is very much the condition of Early's army as an army."

PRE-OWNED PRESIDENTIAL

As the President prepared to make his daily trek to the War Department next door, a sudden downpour delayed his departure.

He asked a servant to fetch him an umbrella. None could be immediately located. Finally one old rickety one was found in the Executive Mansion basement.

When the servant apologized, Lincoln said, "It reminds me of President Fillmore, just after he succeeded Zachary Taylor, who had died. Well, Fillmore ordered a Presidential carriage, and when one was brought to him, Fillmore looked it over and said, 'But this is not new. Don't you think the President of the United States should merit more than a second-hand carriage?'"

The servant looked at him. "But what are you but a second-hand President?"

PRESIDENTIAL POLISH

Class is more than a matter of breeding—it is that of behavior.

When Secretary of Treasury Salmon Chase saw Abraham Lincoln shining his own shoes in his White House office, he asked, "Mr. President, why are you blacking your own shoes?"

Lincoln responded, "Whose shoes would you have me black, Mr. Secretary?"

"THE PRICE IS RIGHT"

Right after Lincoln was awarded the presidential nomination in Chicago, party officials rushed the fifty-one-year-old Springfield lawyer to a photographer. Woodcuts of the photograph were needed to distribute to newspapers and party organizations around the country.

Despite the fact that the photo showed a harried Lincoln with straggly unkempt hair, the photo was sent out. The next day Lincoln heard outside his hotel a vendor hawking his picture.

"Get a picture of Abe Lincoln cheap—cost is only one bit—when Abe gets his hair slicked down for the next picture it will cost you two bits."

PRINCIPLES OF PULCHRITUDE

In the spring of 1864, a delegation from the Union League of Philadelphia called on President Lincoln. The organization was established by influential Philadelphians to support the policies of Lincoln. They had commissioned an artist named Marchant to paint a portrait of the President. Marchant had been staying at the White House for months working on the portrait. Now that the painting was completed, three members of the Union League came to inspect the work.

The painting imparted a measure of nobility to Lincoln's homely features. Lincoln looked at it and said to the artist in the presence of the Union League visitors: "I presume in painting your beautiful portrait, you took your idea from my principles and not from my person."

PROCESS OF ELIMINATION

President Lincoln was asked what he thought of General William Tecumseh Sherman, whose "scorched-earth campaign" from Savannah to Athens had struck fear in the hearts of Georgians.

Lincoln said he was reminded of the time Ethan Allen visited Britain after the War of Independence. The Revolutionary general was hosted by an English earl. As Allen went to the manor's outhouse to perform his morning ablutions, he noted that a picture of General George Washington had been stuck on the door facing the seat. Afterward the earl asked Allen for his reaction.

"Well, Your Lordship, I think the picture is a pretty good method to effect movement. For seeing George Washington would scare the shit out of any Englishman."

PROMISSORY "VOTE"

Clement Vallandingham was, perhaps, the most prominent Copperhead in the Civil War. (Copperheads were Northerners who openly sided with the Confederacy.) Vallandingham, governor of Ohio, was forced to flee to Canada in 1863, and his wife told her friends that she expected never to return until she did so as the wife of the governor of Ohio.

When Lincoln was told of her vow, he said, "That reminds me of a little affair that occurred out in Illinois. A gentleman was nominated as Supervisor. On leaving home on the morning of election, he said, 'Wife, tonight you shall sleep with the Supervisor of this town.'

"The election took place, and the confident gentleman was defeated. The wife heard the news before her defeated spouse returned home. She immediately dressed for going out, and waited her husband's return, when she met him at the door. 'Wife, where are you going at this time of night?' he exclaimed.

"'Going?' she replied. 'Why, you told me this morning that I should sleep tonight with the Supervisor of this town, and as Mr. Logan is elected instead of yourself, I was going to his house!'"

QUO VADIS?

When Lincoln ran for Congress in 1846 against Reverend Peter Cartwright, that Methodist hellfire-and-damnation evangelist spread the word that Lincoln was a "godless atheist."

Lincoln went to a revival meeting in Springfield, where Cartwright said, "All who wish to go to heaven shall stand." Everybody but Lincoln stood. Cartwright then said, "All who do not wish to go to hell shall stand." Again everybody but Lincoln rose. "I observe," said the preacher candidate, "that everybody but Mr. Lincoln has indicated he did not want to go to hell. May I inquire of you, Mr. Lincoln, where you are going?"

"Brother Cartwright asks me directly where I am going. My answer is, I am going to Congress."

REAR VIEW

Ward Hill Lamon was not only a legal colleague but a close friend of Lincoln's. Just before going to court for a case Lamon was trying in Springfield, he split the seat of his pants.

Another lawyer passed around a hat asking for contributions to buy Lamon a new pair of trousers.

Lincoln, instead of a dollar, dropped a note into the hat, saying, "I can contribute nothing to the end in view."

REBEL RACCOON

When Lee surrendered to Grant at Appomattox Court House in Virginia, the question of what to do with the Confederacy's president, Jefferson Davis, posed a tricky problem for Lincoln. Although some radical Republicans were gleefully singing the Union Army ditty "Hang Jeff Davis on an Old Apple Tree," Lincoln thought any martyrdom status for the Southern leader would only exacerbate the difficulties of Reconstruction.

To one adviser who told the President that Davis was preparing an escape, Lincoln said it reminded him of a Springfield lad who adopted a baby raccoon whose mother had been killed while attacking chickens.

The boy loved his "coon" but the feelings weren't reciprocated. One morning he was sighted coming down the road. A fellow townsman coming up the street observed that the boy's face was bloody with scratches, his shirt torn to shreds, and his pants ripped.

The neighbor said, "Son, you got to do something about that coon of yours."

The youth replied, "I know he's been chewing up my clothes. In fact right now he's chewing on his leash—when he chews that through, I'll just let that coon go."

ROAD RUNNER

In the summer of 1861, a large contingent of congressmen made the four-hour journey from Washington to Manassas, Virginia, to observe the first military engagement of troops with the Confederacy. Their carriages were packed with picnic lunches and bottles of wine. It was to be a gala spectacle, since everyone figured that the ensuing battle would be a rout of the Confederacy.

The first Battle of Bull Run, however, proved to be a debacle for the Union Army. One visitor who had been at Manassas recounted how a terrorized congressman had hightailed it up the dirt road in front of the advancing Confederates.

Said Lincoln, "I know what you mean. I once saw a man run like that. He was courting a young girl whose father took such a dislike of him that he threatened to shoot him if he ever caught him on his premises.

"One night just when the young suitor had an arm around the girl's waist about to kiss her, he suddenly spied her father coming around the house with a shotgun.

"Leaping through the window into the garden, he started down the path at the top of his speed like greased lightning. Just then a jackrabbit jumped into the path in front of him. In about two leaps, the young man overtook the rabbit. Giving it a kick that sent it high in the air he yelled, 'Git out of the road, gosh dern you and let somebody runs that knows how.'"

ROGUE ELEPHANT

As the war was ending in April 1865, the Union Army caught the former Confederate envoy to Canada in Maine as he was boarding a British ship from Halifax, Nova Scotia, to escape to London. A telegram to the White House asked the President what his disposition was regarding the Confederate prisoner.

Lincoln, thinking of both future Reconstruction problems as well as diplomatic confrontations with the British, wired back:

"When you got an elephant by the hind leg, and he is trying to run away, it's best to let him run."

"ROLL OUT THE BARREL . . . "

In one of the Lincoln-Douglas debates, Stephen Douglas tried to ingratiate himself with the working people of his audience by confiding that his father had been a cooper and that at one time he had been an apprentice to his father, learning the trade of making barrels.

Lincoln pointed to his short and rotund opponent, whose weight was no doubt enhanced by his love of liquor, and said:

"My distinguished opponent's father must have been a master craftsman because he certainly fashioned here a very fine whiskey keg."

RUNNING SCARED

A judge came to Lincoln one day with the case of a soldier convicted of desertion. "This soldier does not deny his guilt," summarized the military judge, "and it is my recommendation that he will serve the country better dead than living."

Lincoln deliberated for a while and then turned to the judge. "Well, after all, Judge," he said, "I think I'll just have to put this matter with my 'leg cases.'"

"Leg cases?" cried the military magistrate. "What do you mean by 'leg cases' sir?"

"Why, Judge," said Lincoln, "do you see those papers crowded into those pigeonholes? They are cases that you legally describe as 'cowardice in the face of the enemy,' but I call them for short my 'leg cases.' I put it to you, and I leave it for you to decide for yourself: if Almighty God gives a man a cowardly pair of legs, how can he help their running away with him?"

SAD UNDERTAKING

A ranking official of the Post Office died and the next day a job applicant waylaid President Lincoln in the White House.

"Mr. President, did you know that the Chief Postal Inspector just died. Can I take his place?"

"Well," drawled Lincoln, "it's all right with me if it's all right with the undertaker."

SECOND COMING

In the presidential campaign of 1860 Lincoln was asked if he thought Senator Stephen Douglas would return to stage another debate at the state fair. He said it reminded him of a preacher who wanted to use the House legislative chamber in the Springfield Capitol for a sermon.

The Speaker of the House asked what would be the title of his talk.

The clergyman answered, "My title will be 'The Second Coming.'"

"Well, I don't know," replied the Illinois legislator. "If the Lord had ever been here in Springfield, He would never want to come back here a second time."

"SEE NO EVIL . . . "

South Carolina seceded from the Union in April 1861. The South Carolina commissioner appointed by the new government asked to meet with President Lincoln.

Lincoln replied, "I have no eyes but constitutional eyes—I cannot see you."

THE SHORT AND LONG OF IT

A petty bureaucrat had submitted to Lincoln a recommendation. At the end of it the official had signed his name large with ornate swirls and sweeping flourishes.

Lincoln showed the signature to a visitor and said it reminded him of a short-legged man he knew back in Illinois who always wore a big overcoat, the tail of which was so long it wiped out his footprints in the snow as he walked.

SHORT AND SWEET

After Lincoln was nominated by the Republican convention in Chicago in 1860, a newspaper wrote to him asking for an interview in order that they would write the story of his life.

Lincoln answered, "My life is contained in one line of Thomas Gray's 'Elegy Written in a Country Church Yard': 'the short and simple annals of the poor.'"

SICK LIST

Nothing exasperated President Lincoln more than the problem of patronage. A congressman came in to see Lincoln one day to press him to name his friend commissioner of the Sandwich (Hawaiian) Islands.

"Mr. President," the politician urged, "this man toiled hard for you as President in the 1860 campaign but now he is in frail condition. The climate of those Pacific islands would do much to restore his health."

Replied Lincoln, "Congressman, there are eight other applicants and they are all sicker than your man."

SLIM PICKINGS

In his debate in 1858 with Lincoln for his reelection to the U.S. Senate, Stephen Douglas had more at stake than his Senate seat. He was the leading candidate for the Democratic presidential nomination for 1860. Yet, as a Northerner, Douglas could not afford to alienate the Southern wing of his party.

As his opponent, Lincoln targeted what would be his opponent's Achilles' heel. It was Douglas's advocacy of "Popular Sovereignty." That doctrine would, in effect, negate the Fugitive Slave Law in the Territories. A Territory that chose to be "free" could reject the statutory obligation to return fleeing slaves.

When Douglas tried to reconcile the philosophical inconsistencies, Lincoln answered that the Senator's logic was as "thin as the homeopathic soup that was made by baking the shadow of a pigeon that had been starved to death."

SOCK IT TO HIM

While President-elect Lincoln was calling upon the governor in Springfield, an old lady entered, saying, "I want to give the new President a gift."

As she gave Lincoln a pair of wool socks to wear at his inaugural, she confided, "I knitted these myself, Mr. Lincoln."

When she left, Lincoln hung up the stockings by their toes and looked them up and down.

"The old lady," said Lincoln, "got my latitude and longitude just about right, didn't she?"

SOLON SOPHISTRY

In his debates with Stephen Douglas in 1858 for the U.S. Senate, Lincoln repeatedly tried to nail his opponent on the inconsistency of his "Popular Sovereignty" doctrine.

To retain his Southern supporters, Douglas said he supported the Fugitive Slave Law, which stated that escaping slaves in free territory were property to be returned to their owners. Yet his Popular Sovereignty plan would allow each Territory to choose whether or not to be a "free" or a "slave" state. Lincoln argued that a Territory under Douglas's plan could then reject enforcing the Fugitive Slave Law.

As Douglas struggled to bridge the contradiction, Lincoln mocked the tortured reasoning of his political foe: "Explanations, explanatory, of things explained."

SOMETHING IN COMMON

After a Cabinet officer complained to Lincoln of a political favor he had just given to a Democrat, a visitor to the White House asked the President, "What is your definition of a friend?"

Lincoln stroked his beard reflectively before he answered, "One who has the same enemies you have."

SORE WINNER?

A political ally reported to Lincoln a speech of an abolitionist senator which excorciated his presidency. Lincoln's response was a shrug.

"How can you be so indifferent?" asked his supporter.

Lincoln answered, "It reminds me of a man I knew in Springfield who was henpecked by his wife.

"His neighbor spoke up for the badgered husband when everyone else in the community ridiculed him.

"Then one day his friend witnessed the meek man run from his whip-brandishing virago of a wife.

"His erstwhile supporter said, 'Jones, I've stood up for you but any man who takes a beating from his wife deserves to be horse-whipped.'

"The man smiled. 'Why it didn't hurt so much and you've no idea what a power of good it did for my wife.'"

SPOON RIVER

A Union Army private somehow slipped past Lincoln's aides to the President's office. "Mr. President," he said, "I'm tired of the infantry, I'd like to be with the Quartermaster's Corp."

"No, my man, go away!" replied Lincoln. "I cannot attend to every personal whim. I could just as easily bail out the Potomac with a spoon."

STANDING GRUDGE

When the Confederate commissioners to Britain and France were taken off the British ship *Trent*, Prime Minister Palmerston threatened war. During the subsequent negotiations, Secretary of State Seward recommended to Lincoln that the Union had better deliver up the prisoners.

Lincoln was disgusted with the British, who piously proclaimed their opposition to slavery but nevertheless were politically favoring the Confederates for the commercial advantages to be reaped with expanded trade to the South.

He said, "Seward, I feel a good deal like the sick man in Illinois who was told he probably hadn't many days longer to live, and that he ought to make peace with any enemies he might have. The man he hated worst of all was a fellow named Brown in the next village and he was sent for.

"In a quivering voice the sick man said that he wanted to die at peace with all his fellow creatures, and he hoped he and Brown could now shake hands and bury all their enmity.

"It wasn't long before Brown melted and gave his hand to his neighbor, and they had a regular love-feast. After a parting that would have softened the coldest heart, Brown had about reached the room door for departure when the sick man rose up on his elbow and yelled, 'But see here, Brown, if I should happen to get well, mind that old grudge stands!'"

STRAIGHT TALK

In 1864, a contingent of Confederate cavalry launched a surprise sortie on the nation's capital. In the northeast section of the city many of Washington's officialdom gathered to watch the Union forces repel the raid. In the brief skirmish the captain of a Union company sighted a man standing in the Confederate line of fire.

The Union officer screamed, "Will that damned fool in the stovepipe hat get down?"

President Lincoln immediately obeyed. Later he came over to ask the officer his name. "Oliver Wendell Holmes, sir, from Massachusetts," replied the embarrassed future Supreme Court justice.

"Captain Holmes," said Lincoln, "I want to congratulate you.

Finally I've found someone who knows how to speak straight to his President."

STRANGE BEDFELLOWS?

In his debate with Lincoln, Douglas tried to pin the abolitionist tag on Lincoln. Lincoln was opposed to the spread of slavery in the Territories, but was no abolitionist. Lincoln explained to the audience his position with this analogy.

"If I saw a rattlesnake crawling in the road, any man would say I might seize the nearest stick and kill it; but if I found that rattlesnake in bed with my children, that would be another question."

As his listeners chuckled, he continued, "I might hurt the children more than the snake, because it might bite them."

As more of the audience laughed, Lincoln went on to say, "Furthermore, if I found it in bed with my neighbor's children, and I had bound myself by a solemn compact not to meddle with his children under any circumstances, it would oblige me not to be involved.

"But if there was a bed newly made up," Lincoln explained further, "to which the children were to be taken, and it was proposed to take a batch of little rattlers and put them there with them, no one would say there was any question how I ought to decide!"

SUPINE SURPLUS

General George McClellan's repeated answer to Lincoln's charges of delay was that he did not have enough troops. When a friend of McClellan relayed another request for more men to the President, Lincoln replied:

"If I give McClellan all the men he asks for, they could not find men room to lie down, they'd have to sleep standing up."

TAIL END

Lincoln once represented a client indicted for assault and battery. Lincoln argued that it was self-defense. Lincoln told the jury that his client was in the plight of a man who, in going along the highway with a pitchfork over his shoulder, was attacked by a fierce dog that ran out at him from a farmer's dooryard. He warded off the beast with his pitchfork and one of its prongs pierced and killed it. In his summary to the jury, Lincoln recounted the exchange between the two men.

"What made you kill my dog?" said the cur's owner.

"What made him bite me?" replied the pitchforker.

"But why did you not go after him with the other end of the pitchfork?" asked the dead dog's master.

Lincoln's client answered, "And why did he not come at me with his other end?"

At this Mr. Lincoln got down on his knees, whirled, and pushed his rear end toward the jury box as its members laughed. An acquittal was the result.

"TAKE [A] WIFE, PLEASE"

John Fremont, the Republican candidate for President in 1856, wanted to be made a Union Army general, but Lincoln had his doubts about the outspoken Fremont's habit of shooting from the hip. Yet his radical Republican backers were adamant in demanding a generalship for the abolitionist hero. Lincoln explained that to give

Fremont a command would mean that another general would have to be removed.

Lincoln said that to appoint Fremont reminded him of the old man who told his son to take a wife. The son asked, "Whose wife shall I take?"

TALL "TAIL"

Some of Lincoln's advisers came to the White House to urge him to issue an edict proclaiming that all the slaves were free. Lincoln insisted that saying slaves were free would not make them free. To explain, he asked, "If you call a sheep's tail a leg, how many legs does a sheep have?"

"Five," the advisers agreed.

"No," replied Lincoln. "A sheep only has four legs." Then Lincoln added, "Calling a tail a leg doesn't make it so."

TANGLE-LEGS

If Lincoln's hand could pen elegant prose, his long legs lacked a similar grace. At a Springfield soiree, the courting Lincoln edged over to the silk-gowned Mary Todd and offered, "Miss Mary, I'd like to dance with you in the worst way."

After a spin on the floor, Mary said, "Abraham, you wanted to dance in the worst way and you certainly did!"

TERRIBLE TRIO

Of the radical Republicans, the three who were the sharpest thorns in Lincoln's side were Senators Henry Wilson and Charles Sumner of Massachusetts and Congressman Thaddeus Stevens of Pennsylvania.

As President Lincoln was recounting his difficulties with the radical Republicans, he looked out the window of his office and saw the three striding up Pennsylvania Avenue for a meeting. Lincoln said he was reminded of a recitation when he was a nine-year-old schoolboy.

The schoolmaster would open the Bible for reading and each would have to read aloud one verse in a passage from Scripture. On this day the teacher opened to Daniel. Each pupil took his turn, but for one boy the verse included the three biblical names of Shadrach, Mischach, and Abednego. The unfortunate lad struggled with the names and sat down.

Minutes later his turn had come again and to his dismay the verse he had to recite included the same three jawbreakers.

He stood up and sighed aloud to the class. "Here comes those dang three again."

And Lincoln added, pointing out the window, "And right now I can say the same thing."

TEST CASE

When Congress enacted a tax on state-chartered banks, Lincoln expressed his belief that it was a prelude to taxing national banks.

Lincoln said it reminded him of a farm family he knew in Illinois that had three sons including one moronic youth named Jake.

One day the whole family took sick after eating spinach.

The next week when more spinach was picked, the father said, "Let's give it to Jake first. If he don't take sick we can all eat it."

"THIS IS WHERE I GET OFF . . . "

General George McClellan, the head of the Army of the Potomac, if slow to engage the Confederates in battle, was quick to give his commander in chief advice on how to run the nation. Governor John Andrew of Indiana asked Lincoln what he thought of McClellan's advice.

Lincoln answered, "Nothing—but it makes me think of the man whose horse kicked up and stuck his foot through the stirrup. He said to the horse, 'If you are going to get on, I'm going to get off.'"

TILL HELL FREEZES OVER

At one Cabinet meeting the President put his suggested policy up for consideration. Every member of the Cabinet spoke out against the Lincoln view. His minority position, said Lincoln, reminded him of a revival meeting in Illinois when a fellow with a few drinks too many in him walked up the aisle to a front pew. All eyes were on him, but he didn't care. He joined in the singing, droning "Amen" at the close of prayers, and as the meeting proceeded, dozed off in sleep. Before the meeting ended, the pastor asked the usual question: "Who are on the Lord's side?" and the congregation arose except the sot.

When the pastor asked, "Who are on the side of Satan?" the napping congregant awoke. Though he heard only part of the question, he could see the parson was standing. So he arose to his feet to say: "I don't exactly understand the question but I'll stand by you, parson, to the last. But it seems to me," he added reflectively, "that we're in a hopeless minority."

TIP-TOP

A dozen or more leading businessmen from Wilmington, Delaware, called on Lincoln one day.

"Mr. President," said the chairman of the delegation, "we are all the top leaders—you might say that we represent the weight of Delaware."

When their spokesman completed his little speech, Lincoln asked, "So you are the weighty men of Delaware? All from New Castle County."

"Yes," piped up a couple, "we're all from the same city."

"Well," said Lincoln impishly, "did it ever occur to you gentlemen that with all the weight of you three here today, there was danger of your state tipping up in your absence?"

TOO FINE "APPOINT"

Some Republicans came to the White House to ask Lincoln to appoint their political cohort as port collector of Philadelphia.

"Mr. President," said their spokesman, "we have come here today to present our fellow Philadelphian to your favorable consideration. He is eminently qualified for the position—not only for his administrative ability, but also for his unswerving loyalty to the Republican party. No honors, sir," continued the head of the Philadelphia delegation, "could be showered on him that could elevate him higher in the estimation of his fellow-men."

"Gentlemen," said Lincoln with a smile, "it gives me much gratification to hear the praise bestowed. Such a man needs no office—it can confer on him no additional advantage, or add prestige to his well-earned fame!

"Indeed you are right, Mr. Chairman," summed up Lincoln, "that no honors could be showered on him that would elevate him higher in the estimation of his fellow-man. So to appoint so good and excellent a gentlemen to a paltry position like this would be an act of

injustice to him. I shall reserve the office for some poor politician
who needs it."

TOO LAZY TO STOP

Lawyer Lincoln rode horseback to the various county seats
when the circuit court was holding session. As Lincoln awaited
his case, another lawyer gave Judge Davis a many-paged petition
in equity.

Afterward, Judge Davis showed to Lincoln the chancery bill
by the usually sluggish attorney. "A long job, Abe, for such a lazy
man," remarked Judge Davis.

Replied Lincoln, "It's like the lazy preacher I once heard that used
to write long sermons. He got to writing and was too lazy to stop."

TRANSCENDENT TRUTH

After Lincoln's election, an army of job-seekers swarmed upon
the White House. Interviewing them was one presidential job that
Lincoln found most distasteful. Few men have ever possessed the
patience of Lincoln; but even his was taxed on these occasions.
Once, after a particularly unqualified man had just called upon him
for a government job, Lincoln said to his aide John Hay after he
left:

"Well, a ruler once asked his advisors if there was one maxim that
could be truly applied in all times and situations. The advisors
returned and presented him the words: 'And this, too, shall pass
away.'

"How much it expresses," said Lincoln. "How chastening to the
hour of pride! How consoling in the depths of affliction."

TUMMY TONIC?

In the spring of 1864, Lincoln took a ride down the Potomac on a river steamer. When the river became choppy, the captain advised, "Mr. President, the best cure for seasickness is champagne. It really settles the stomach."

Lincoln shook his head and replied, "No thanks, I've seen too many people get seasick on land from drinking that stuff."

"UNEASY LIES THE HEAD . . . "

In a Lincoln campaign for reelection to the Illinois legislature, he tangled in debate with one George Forquer, a onetime Whig who had changed his politics to Democrat in order to receive a prize appointment from President Andrew Jackson. With his handsome new emolument, Forquer had a mansion built, topped with a lighting rod.

In the debate, Forquer brutally savaged the young Lincoln. When it was Lincoln's turn to speak, he replied to Forquer's argument clearly and effectively. Then he paused—and with cutting sarcasm launched an attack on his opponent.

"Among other things, my opponent in this debate has said that 'this young man,' alluding to me, 'must be taken down.' I am not so young in years as I am in tricks of the trade of a politician, but," Lincoln said, pointing a deadly finger at Forquer, "live long or die young, I would rather die now than, like the gentleman, change my politics and with it receive an office worth three thousand dollars a year and then feel obligated to erect a lightning rod over my house to protect a guilty conscience from an offended God."

UNLIMITED LARGESSE

One day President Lincoln woke up ill running a fever. Still he went to his office to receive visitors. An office seeker came in just as the President's physician happened to enter the room.

Lincoln held out his hand to show some speckled blotches and said, "Doctor, what are these?"

Replied his doctor, "That's varioloid, a mild form of small pox."

"Is it contagious?" asked the President.

"Oh yes, very contagious."

"Well, that's good Doctor," said Lincoln as the doctor left. "Now I have something I can give to everybody."

With that Lincoln grinned as his physician departed.

"WALKING DEAD"

Democrat Stephen Douglas came to the state fair in 1854 at Springfield to advance his candidacy for the U.S. Senate. It was there that he first heard that Lincoln was attacking his championship of the Kansas-Nebraska Act.

Although Douglas was actually well acquainted with Lincoln, he pretended otherwise, publicly sneering at the mention of his name.

"I understand there's some Whig lawyer around here taking issue with me—doesn't he know that the Whig Party is dead?"

The next day Lincoln agreed to oppose Douglas in debate, representing those against the Kansas-Nebraska Act.

Lincoln opened his remarks saying, "I understand Judge Douglas said the Whigs are dead. Well if that's the case, I ask the band to play that familiar 'Hark from the Tombs, a Doleful Sound,' because as I live and breathe, I'm here to speak."

THE WALNUT WAR

A visitor to Lincoln's White House office noted that his two sons were fighting with each other. He asked what they were quarreling about.

Lincoln replied, "Just what's wrong with the whole world. I've got three walnuts in my hand and each wants two."

WASTE MATTER?

After repeated requests by President Lincoln, General George McClellan reluctantly began to deploy the Army of the Potomac southward into Virginia.

When his slow movements were reported, Lincoln sighed in exasperation. "What is the matter with McClellan?" he asked rhetorically to an aide. Then he added, "Why his troops move as slowly as fleas across a barnyard of shit."

WONDER WOMAN

Once when Lincoln heard criticism of his wife, he allowed that none of us is perfect—"even our wives." He then told of a southern Illinois preacher who, in the course of his sermon, asserted that the Savior was the only perfect man who had ever appeared in this world; and that there was no record, in the Bible or elsewhere, of any perfect woman having lived on the earth.

Whereupon there came from the rear of the church a mousy woman whose harrowed look and hesitant voice said, "Begging your pardon, I know a perfect woman, Reverend, and I've heard of her every day for the last six years."

"Who was she?" asked the minister.

Replied the downtrodden woman, "My husband's first wife."

WRITE AND IGNITE

One morning Edwin Stanton, Lincoln's secretary of war, stormed into the President's office. Stanton was angry at a letter a major general had written him.

Lincoln told him to write him back a letter. At the President's desk Stanton sat down to write.

"Stick it to him," egged on Lincoln, and Stanton penned on furiously.

"Scorch the General," urged the President, and the war secretary continued to vent his rage on paper. "Really scold him," Lincoln pressed.

When Stanton finally finished, Lincoln took the letter and tore it up.

"Why did you do that?" questioned a perplexed Stanton.

"You don't want to send that letter, Stanton. Put it in the stove." Lincoln continued, "That's what I do when I've written a letter when I'm angry. It's a humdinger of a letter and you've had a hell of a good time writing it. Now burn it and write another letter."

Abe's Addresses

If there is one central theme that permeates Abraham Lincoln's speeches, it is the Declaration of Independence. On Washington's birthday in 1861, Lincoln, as President-elect, pointed to Independence Hall and said, "I have never had a political feeling that did not spring from the sentiments embodied in the Declaration of Independence."

The sincerity of those words by a politician today might be dismissed as the typical bombast heard on a patriotic observance. Yet Lincoln, who disdained political cant, rarely indulged in rhetorical excess. He was merely expressing the central core of his beliefs. To Lincoln those words "all men are created equal" were a God-revealed truth.

Today we assume that the words "all men are created equal" have been etched in the hearts of Americans ever since the day the Continental Congress passed the Resolves in 1776. But look at the name of Jefferson's manifesto: "Declaration of Independence"—not "Declaration of Equality."

The Fourth of July was a holiday to celebrate our independence from Britain and the birth of our nation. But to Lincoln the philosophy of Jefferson's natural rights transcended the nationhood of America.

Other countries—such as the Netherlands against Spain—had freed themselves from colonial rule. It was the idea of democracy that made America different. As a document, the Constitution—not the Declaration—was the charter which politicians most invoked in the early nineteenth century. Lincoln, as a legislator, lawyer, and then as President, revered the Constitution as the organic framework of our laws and government. But if the significance of the Constitution was legal applying just to our national body of laws, the Declaration of Independence was universal—offering hope to the world.

For that reason Jefferson was the Founding Father whom Lincoln most honored—even more than the sainted George Washington. Yet Jefferson was late entering the American pantheon of select heroes. In the first years of our Republic, Jefferson was viewed as a partisan figure. After all, he was the father of the Democratic party. Democrats still continue to celebrate Jefferson-Jackson Day Dinners as the Republicans do the Lincoln Day Dinners.

It was the Democratic President Franklin Roosevelt who promoted Jefferson to the Olympian heights of Washington and Lincoln to cement his political axis to the Southern Democrats. That was why he had the Jefferson Memorial built and Jefferson's face engraved on the nickel.

For most of his political career, Lincoln was a Whig, and the Whigs' hero was General George Washington. That explains why the Whig party often sought out generals to be their standard-bearers (Harrison, Taylor, Scott) in the hope of recapturing the aura of a Washington—a President who kept himself remote from the partisan politics of Congress.

If Jefferson was Lincoln's philosopher, Henry Clay was his "beau ideal" politician. As a native Kentuckian, Lincoln could identify with the legendary lawyer legislator from the same state.

Lincoln had a scrapbook in which the Declaration of Independence by Jefferson was affixed. Beneath it Lincoln had printed out the words of Clay saying, "No earthly power will make me vote directly or indirectly to spread slavery over territory where it does not exist."

Lincoln never established himself as a distinguished orator like Clay. The backwoods folk who were Lincoln's audiences in jury trials and stump speeches might have looked askance at any attempt by Lincoln into flights of rhetoric. Lincoln had too much common sense to make such a mistake. If his early delivery had been halting, he grew more self-confident by honing his own style of plain talk that was brightened by homey analogies and droll stories.

As a trial lawyer, Lincoln perfected this folksy persuasion in countless appeals to backwoods juries. By the time of his debates with Stephen Douglas, Lincoln had turned his handicap of education and lack of forensic elegance into a political asset.

In a sense, the Lincoln-Douglas debates not only pitted two different approaches to freedom (Lincoln's opposition to the territorial extension of slavery against Douglas's Popular Sovereignty) but two different styles of speaking: Lincoln the country lawyer against Douglas the senatorial orator.

Douglas won the election by winning more votes from the Illinois state legislators, but Lincoln received more votes from the people of Illinois. (The legislative candidates pledged to Lincoln actually received more votes than the Douglas candidates but more Douglas men were elected.)

Only a few times in his life did Lincoln attempt the rhetorical style favored by the learned of his day. The first time was in his speech to the Lyceum in 1838. Some of the language of that address comes close to purpled prose. The twenty-nine-year-old Lincoln, who was accepting his first prestigious invitation to a public address, probably felt he had to fashion a more ornate and fervid style to impress his audience. If it was a mistake, it is one that inexperienced speakers often make.

Yet Lincoln came to realize that an address at a state function or a ceremonial occasion demanded more than a folksy dialogue and funny stories. His first hint of this was his eulogy of Henry Clay in 1852. By the time of the Gettysburg Address a decade later, Lincoln had attained the heights of sublime eloquence.

In the following century, Lincoln would replace Daniel Webster as a paradigm for American students of rhetoric. His Gettysburg Address and Second Inaugural Address offered up language that imparted the Elizabethan majesty of Shakespeare and the King James Bible. Still, if the choice of words was stately, the structure was simple.

Like Churchill in the future, Lincoln would shun the passive voice and Latin polysyllabics, but Lincoln avoided also the Churchill flourishes of adverbial beginnings (Never in the history . . . . Not for the first time) and his Gibbonian emulation of "not only's" and "but also's." The end result was a nobility as well as an economy of language.

The progression from a backwoods practioner of law to a presidential "poet" was not overnight. A reader of Lincoln's prepared addresses need only study his Lyceum Speech in 1838 and the Gettysburg Address a quarter of a century later to observe the evolution.

The Lincoln style—at least in his prepared addresses—changed, but the substance of his principles did not. Lincoln always believed that America was unique—that like the Israel of the Bible, God had made America a "chosen land."

The Declaration of Independence was his scripture. Yet it was not until the Lincoln-Douglas debate that Lincoln was forced to spell out his political philosophy. His speeches afterward—the Cooper Union speech, the remarks at Independence Hall in 1861, his presidential message to Congress in 1862—all mark the way to Gettysburg.

❧ ❧ ❧

FIRST CANDIDACY ANNOUNCEMENT (March 1832)

In 1832, Lincoln made his first political bid. The twenty-three-year-old store clerk announced his candidacy as a Whig to represent Sangamon County in the Illinois State Legislature. Though he garnered ninety percent of the vote in his hometown of New Salem, he would lose the election.

In an open letter to the citizens of Sangamon County, Lincoln would outline his program to foster education, morality, and religious values. ("The advantages and satisfaction to be derived from all of being able to read the scriptures and other works both of a reli-

gious and moral nature.") He closed on a personal note that reflect-
ed his self-effacing style:

☞ I am young and unknown to many of you. I was born and have
ever remained in the most humble walks of life. I have no wealthy
or popular relations to recommend me. My case is thrown exclusively upon the independent voters of this County and if elected that
will have conferred a favor upon me for which I shall be unremitting
in my labors to compensate. But if the people in their wisdom shall
see fit to keep me in the background, I have been too familiar with
disappointments to be very much chagrined. ☜

YOUNG MEN'S LYCEUM ADDRESS (January 12, 1838)

In 1838, the twenty-nine-year-old Lincoln received his first prestigious speech invitation. Lincoln at the time had been practicing
law for two years and serving as a state legislator for four years. As
one of the "Long Nine," Lincoln was one of the Whig party's most
active members in the State House. (The Long Nine referred to a
young group of activists, all of whom were over six feet.) His
increased standing in the community had prompted the invitation.

The recent killing of an abolitionist editor, Elijah Lovejoy, in
Alton, Illinois, moved Lincoln to prepare an address that denounced
mob protest and upheld the rule of law. Far from his measured and
majestic prose of his presidential years, Lincoln indulged in some
passionate rhetoric to impress his upscale audience:

☞ Let every American, every lover of liberty, every well wisher to
his posterity, swear by the blood of the Revolution, never to violate
in the least particular, the laws of the country; and never to tolerate

their violation by others. As the patriots of seventy-six did to the support of the Declaration of Independence, so to the support of the Constitution and Laws, let every American pledge his life, his property, and his sacred honor;—let every man remember that to violate the law, is to trample on the blood of his father, and to tear the character of his own, and his children's liberty.

Let reverence for the laws, be breathed by every American mother, to the lisping babe, that prattles on her lap—let it be taught in schools, in seminaries, and in colleges;—let it be written in Primers, spelling books, and in Almanacs;—let it be preached from the pulpit, proclaimed in legislative halls, and enforced in courts of justice. And, in short, let it become the political religion of the nation. 📖1

"SPOT" RESOLUTION (March 1848)

For a freshman congressman to introduce a resolution attacking the President of the United States on his decision to wage war was almost tantamount to treason.

Lincoln harbored no pacifist qualms—as his presidency some decades later would prove. Lincoln, however, was troubled by President Polk's grounds for invading Mexico.

Lincoln introduced his "Eight Spot Resolutions" intending to force Polk to admit that Mexico and not the United States held jurisdiction on the "spot" where the war started. Many Whigs in the North shared Lincoln's fears that war waged by the Tennesseean Polk was at least partially motivated by the desire to extend slavery to the southwest United States. Rare was the politician who dared to attack openly the President on a generally popular war against Mexico in a time when Polk's "Manifest Destiny" echoed Americans' continental ambitions.

For Lincoln, it was a matter of conscience. This politically unpopular act was one reason Lincoln did not choose to run for reelection. The first three of the Resolutions are enough to explain that the first bloodshed happened on Mexican territory.

☞ First: Whether the spot of soil on which the blood of our citizens was shed, as in his messages declared, was, or was not, within the territories of Spain, at least from the treaty of 1819 until the Mexican revolution.

Second: Whether that spot is, or is not, within the territory which was wrested from Spain, by the Mexican revolution.

Third: Whether that spot is, or is not, within a settlement of people, which settlement had existed ever since long before that Texas Revolution, until its inhabitants fled from the approach of the U.S. Army. . . . ☜

HENRY CLAY EULOGY (July 6, 1852)

Henry Clay, one of the greatest senators in American history, died in 1852. The Whig party leader, who thrice lost a presidential election, once said, "I'd rather be right than President." Lincoln called Clay "the beau ideal of a statesman." Lincoln was born in Kentucky and grew up idolizing the Kentucky orator who became a senator the year Lincoln was born.

At a memorial meeting in Springfield, Lincoln delivered a eulogy to his hero. Lincoln, while still an active Whig, had in 1852 given up his political ambitions and was concentrating on building his legal practice.

In his lament for Clay, Lincoln was unconsciously voicing his regrets for his own departure from a political career. He was also pondering the future of American democracy. Clay died at age seventy-five—five years beyond the biblical span of three score and ten. Clay and America were almost the same age. How long will democracy endure? was Lincoln's implicit question.

☞ On the fourth day of July, 1776, the people of a few feeble and oppressed colonies of Great Britain, publicly declared their national independence, and made their appeal to the justice of their cause, and to the God of battles, for the maintenance of that declaration.

Within the first year of that declared independence, . . . Henry Clay was born. The infant nation, and the infant child began the race of life together. For three quarters of a century they have travelled hand in hand. They have been companions ever. The nation has passed its perils, and is free, prosperous, and powerful. The child has reached his manhood, his middle age, his old age, and is dead. In all that has concerned the nation the man ever sympathized; and now the nation mourns for the man. ☜

KANSAS-NEBRASKA ACT SPEECH (October 11, 1854)

The passage of the Kansas-Nebraska Act in 1854 was an alarm that wakened Lincoln from a self-imposed retirement to political action. As Lincoln wrote later, "I was losing interest when the repeal of the Missouri Compromise aroused me again."

Though Lincoln had not yet left the Whig party to join the fledgling Republicans, his decision to debate Douglas at Peoria in October would culminate in his leadership of the "Anti-Nebraskans." The

Douglas bill that would open up the question of slavery in the Territories was the core issue that was splitting the Whig and Democratic parties.

Lincoln would follow the three-hour address of Judge Douglas with a speech almost as long. It would attack Douglas's theory of Popular Sovereignty.

Lincoln would assert that he had no prejudice against Southern people and their constitutional right to own slaves, and stressed that he only opposed the extension of slavery while "the little giant," as Douglas was called, would further its spread. Douglas's advocacy of Popular Sovereignty was a rehearsed oration only relieved by histrionic asides as well as some sardonic comments about his opponent. If Lincoln was more the plainspoken, his style also ran the gamut from broad humor to moral outrage:

☞ The doctrine of self government is right—absolutely and eternally right—but it has no just application, as here attempted. Or perhaps I should rather say that whether it has such just application depends upon whether a negro is not or is a man. If he is not a man, why in that case, he who is a man may, as a matter of self-government, do just as he pleases with him. But if the negro is a man, is it not to that extent, a total destruction of self-government, to say that he too shall not govern himself?

When the white man governs himself that is self-government; but when he governs himself, and also governs another man, that is more than self-government—that is despotism [italics mine]. If the negro is a man, why then my ancient faith teaches me that "all men are created equal;" and that there can be no moral right in connection with one man's making a slave of another. ☜

"HOUSE DIVIDED" SPEECH (July 12, 1858)

At the state Republican convention in Springfield in July 1858, Lincoln was named as the Republican candidate for the U.S. Senate. He opened his speech with a direct challenge to the Kansas-Nebraska Act and its effect on the extension of slavery in the Territories.

The speech has become famous for his adaption of a biblical quotation: "A House divided against itself cannot stand." That line and the one that follows ("I believe this government cannot long endure permanently half slave and half free") would be exploited by opponents, when he ran for President two years later, to allege that Lincoln was an extremist with abolitionist leanings. This powerful convention address not only propelled his Senate candidacy but also brought him increasing attention in the Eastern press:

☞ If we could first know where we are, and whither we are tending, we could then better judge what to do, and how to do it.

We are now far into the fifth year, since a policy was initiated, with the avowed object, and confident promise, of putting an end to slavery agitation.

Under the operation of that policy, that agitation has not only, not ceased, but has constantly augmented.

In my opinion, it will not cease, until a crisis shall have been reached, and passed.

A house divided against itself cannot stand.

I believe this government cannot endure, permanently half slave and half free.

I do not expect the Union to be dissolved—I do not expect the house to fall—but I do expect it will cease to be divided.

It will become all one thing, or all the other. ☜

COOPER UNION ADDRESS (February 21, 1866)

By the end of 1859, Lincoln had become a long-shot possibility for the presidency. The Lincoln-Douglas debate, even if the result was a Lincoln defeat, moved him to the front ranks of the Republican party national leaders. On February 16, 1860, the Chicago *Tribune* endorsed Lincoln for President. By that time Lincoln had already accepted an invitation to speak to the Cooper Union Institute. Since he was already planning to take his son Robert east to enroll in Exeter Academy, the speech in New York City meshed with those plans.

Lincoln had no idea that the address would become such a star-spangled occasion. He was escorted to the platform by the noted editor of the New York *Tribune,* Horace Greeley, and was then introduced by the poet William Cullen Bryant. The audience was a Who's Who of the city's elite in art, finance, and industry. They had come to take a look at this prairie lawyer, and he would far surpass their expectations.

Never was Lincoln more nervous about a speech. He feared his backwoods accent would invite ridicule from his urbane listeners. As a result he opened badly in a high-pitched stammer. Soon, though, the conviction of his message made him overcome his self-conscious awkwardness of manner.

The accomplished stump speaker in Lincoln emerged, and his talk demolished the Stephen Douglas thesis that the Founding Fathers had intended to forbid the federal government from controlling slavery in the Territories. On this challenge to prevent the extension of slavery, Lincoln closed with this rousing peroration:

☞ Neither let us be slandered from our duty by false accusations against us, nor frightened from it by menaces of destruction to the

Government nor of dungeons to ourselves. Let us have faith that right makes might, and in that faith, let us, to the end, dare to do our duty as we understand it. ☜

THE FAREWELL ADDRESS IN ILLINOIS (February 11, 1861)
On the day before his fifty-second birthday, Lincoln bade farewell to his longtime friends and supporters at the train station in Springfield. He was about to board the train that would take him to Washington to be inaugurated as the nation's sixteenth President.

If Lincoln was one of the most humble citizens of this Illinois community, he was also the most honored. His few but poignant words bear the premonition that he might never see the people of Springfield again:

☞ My friends—No one, not in my situation, can appreciate my feeling of sadness at this parting. To this place, and the kindness of these people, I owe everything. Here I have lived a quarter of a century, and have passed from a young to an old man. Here my children have been born, and one is buried.

I now leave, not knowing when, or whether ever, I may return, with a task before me greater than that which rested upon Washington. Without the assistance of the Divine Being, who ever attended him, I cannot succeed. With His assistance I cannot fail.

Trusting in Him, who can go with me, and remain with you and be every where for good, let us confidently hope that all will yet be well. To His care commending you, as I hope in your prayers you will commend me, I bid you an affectionate farewell. ☜

INDEPENDENCE HALL REMARKS (February 22, 1861)

The roundabout train journey to Washington that left Springfield on the eve of his birthday would bring Lincoln to Philadelphia on George Washington's birthday. Lincoln made a stop at Independence Hall and was surprised to see the large crowd that had assembled to see him. The occasion thus called for some brief remarks. Though Lincoln spoke extemporaneously, he touched on the idea for the first time that on the success of the American democratic experiment rested the hopes of the world. That theme would later be enshrined by his noble cadences at Gettysburg:

☞ It was not the mere matter of separation of Colonies from the Motherland; but that sentiment in the Declaration of Independence which gave liberty, not alone to the people of this country, but I hope to the world for all future time. It was that which gave promise that in due time the weight would be lifted from the shoulders of all men. ☜

FIRST INAUGURAL (March 4, 1861)

No inaugural address before or since was awaited with such anxiety and interest. Since Lincoln's election in November, the nation was sliding into disunion and inevitable war. Lincoln, whose national experience had been one term in Congress, was an unknown quantity.

Threats on the President-elect's life had forced Lincoln to sneak into the capital city under a cloak of stealth. By March 4, the date of the inaugural, Lincoln had chosen his new Cabinet. His secretary of state-designate was William Seward—still deemed the country's most powerful Republican. Seward, who thought of himself as the "prime minister," had prepared a draft for Lincoln's inaugural address. Seward was miffed by Lincoln's heavy revision.

Lincoln was determined to strike a calm tone for a feverish nation. In his rewording of Seward's stiff and wooden closing, the lyrical style of Lincoln was manifest:

☞ I am loath to close. We are not enemies, but friends. We must not be enemies. Though passion may have strained, it must not break our bonds of affection. The mystic chords of memory, stretching from every battlefield, and patriot grave, to every living heart and hearthstone, all over this broad land, will yet swell the chorus of the Union, when again touched as surely they will be, by the better angels of our nature. ☜

ANNUAL MESSAGE TO CONGRESS (December 3, 1862)

The fall of 1862 brought serious losses to the Republican party. Lincoln responded by replacing the dilatory General McClellan with Ambrose Burnside. On December 1, the President delivered his State of the Union message to the third session of the Thirty-seventh Congress.

His words describing America as "the last best hope of earth" marked the second time Lincoln touched on the theme that would render his Gettysburg Address sublime:

☞ Fellow-citizens, we cannot escape history. We of this Congress and this administration, will be remembered in spite of ourselves. No personal significance, or insignificance, can spare one or another of us. The fiery trial through which we pass, will light us down, in honor or dishonor, to the latest generation. We say we are for the

Union. The world will not forget that we say this. We know how to save the Union. The world knows we do know how to save it. We—even we here—hold the power, and bear the responsibility.

In giving freedom to the slave, we assure freedom to the free—honorable alike in what we give, and what we preserve. We shall nobly save, or meanly lose, the last best hope of earth. Other means may succeed; this could not fail. The way is plain, peaceful, generous, just—a way which, if followed, the world will forever applaud, and God must forever bless. ᴇ⅃

GETTYSBURG ADDRESS (November 19, 1863)

It was the briefest of addresses, but Lincoln would never work more painstakingly on choice of words and phrasing. The battlefield text was the culmination of at least six drafts in two weeks of work in his office at the Executive Mansion.

At the conclusion of Everett's two-hour oration, there was a brief band selection. Then the Marshal Ward Hill Lamon in stentorian tones announced, *"The President of the United States."*

Lincoln removed his stovepipe hat and pulled out the speech he carried in it. He then put on his steel spectacles and began speaking. Although he held the text in his hand, he never glanced at it during his two-minute address. A somewhat tense Lincoln was not as deliberate in pacing as he would have liked. His pitch was tenor and his delivery mostly matter-of-fact. The midwestern nasal twang was neither as stately nor as pretentious as the actors or classroom orators who have imitated him. Yet the evenness of Lincoln's voice would break into emotion as he began "that from these honored dead . . . " The result was a closing that moved his listeners to a reverential awe:

☞ Four score and seven years ago our fathers brought forth on this continent, a new nation, conceived in Liberty, and dedicated to the proposition that all men are created equal.

Now we are engaged in a great civil war, testing whether that nation, or any nation so conceived and so dedicated, can long endure. We are met on a great battlefield of that war. We have come to dedicate a portion of that field, as a final resting place for those who here gave their lives that that nation might live. It is altogether fitting and proper that we should do this.

But, in a larger sense, we cannot dedicate—we cannot consecrate—we cannot hallow—this ground. The brave men, living and dead, who struggled here, have consecrated it, far above our poor power to add or detract. The world will little note, nor long remember what we say here, but it can never forget what they did here. It is for us the living, rather to be dedicated here to the unfinished work which the men who fought here have thus far so nobly advanced. It is rather for us to be here dedicated to the great task remaining before us—that from these honored dead we take increased devotion to that cause for which they gave the last full measure of devotion—that we here highly resolve that these dead shall not have died in vain—that this nation, under God, shall have a new birth of freedom—and that government of the people, by the people, for the people shall not perish from the earth. ☜

SECOND INAUGURAL (March 4, 1865)

If the Gettysburg Address is the most widely known speech in history, Lincoln's Second Inaugural Address contains some of the most sublime prose ever uttered by an American politician, or perhaps by any statesman, not excluding Churchill.

As Grant's army closed in on Richmond, the end of the war was now in sight. For Lincoln, the dominant concern was now the healing that must follow.

The concluding sentence approaches poetry with its iambic pentameter and internal rhyme. In those lyrical lines are the echoes of the Old Testament prescriptions of Isaiah in the King James version of the Bible.

☞ Fondly do we hope—fervently do we pray—that this mighty scourge of war may speedily pass away. Yet if God wills that it continue, until all the wealth piled by the bond-man's two hundred and fifty years of unrequited toil shall be sunk, and until every drop of blood drawn with the lash shall be paid by another drawn with the sword, as was said three thousand years ago, so still it must be said "the judgements of the Lord are true and righteous altogether."

With malice toward none; with charity for all; with firmness in the right, as God gives us to see the right, let us strive on to finish the work we are in; to bind up the nation's wounds; to care for him who shall have borne the battle, and for his widow, and his orphan— to do all which may achieve and cherish a just and a lasting peace, among ourselves and with all nations. ☜

Lincoln's Time Line

HIS LIFE	YEAR	HIS WORLD
Born in a log cabin in Harding County, Kentucky, near Hodgeville—second child of Thomas and Nancy Hanks Lincoln	1809	James Madison sworn in as fourth President; Wellington and British defeat the French in Spain; William Gladstone, the future British prime minister, is born
Family moves to a better farm—230 acres on Knob Creek	1811	King George III declared insane—Regency established; Jane Austen publishes *Sense and Sensibility*
At age seven attends A.B.C. School; family moves again to Spencer County, Indiana	1816	Argentina wins independence from Spain; Rossini writes *The Barber of Seville*
Nancy Hanks Lincoln dies of typhoid	1818	Illinois becomes a state; *Savannah* first steamship to cross Atlantic (twenty-six days)
Thomas Lincoln marries widow Sarah Bush Johnston	1819	Spain cedes Florida to United States; Keats writes "Ode on a Grecian Urn"
Hired out at fifteen by his father for farm work	1824	Greeks fight Turks for independence; Beethoven writes *Ninth Symphony*

HIS LIFE	YEAR	HIS WORLD
Operates a river ferry boat for 37 cents a day at seventeen	1826	Simón Bolívar liberates Colombia, Peru, and Bolivia; James Fenimore Cooper publishes *Last of the Mohicans*
Takes a load of farm produce on a flatboat to New Orleans	1828	General Andrew Jackson elected President; first printing of *Webster's Dictionary*
At age twenty-one moves out of house and gets a job splitting rails	1830	Daniel Webster gives famous speech on the Union in reply to John Calhoun; Bourbon Monarchy falls in France; Louis Philippe new "Citizen King"
Becomes a store clerk in Salem, Illinois	1831	Nat Turner leads slave revolt in New Virginia; Charles Darwin goes as naturalist on H.M.S. *Beagle*
Announces candidacy for state legislature, loses, and serves a few months in Black Hawk War	1832	Poland becomes Russian province; Goethe publishes *Faust*
Appointed postmaster of New Salem, Illinois	1833	Britain abolishes slavery in Empire; Chopin writes piano pieces (Études)
Elected to the Illinois Legislature—borrows $200 for wardrobe and starts to study law	1834	Cyrus McCormick patents his harvesting machine
Ann Rutledge, the love of his life, dies at age twenty-two	1835	Railway boom in Britain; Colt revolver patented in America
Passes bar examination; breaks off engagement to Mary Owens	1836	Texas wins independence from Mexico; de Tocqueville publishes *Democracy in America*

HIS LIFE	YEAR	HIS WORLD
Defeated as Whig leader for Speaker of the House in Illinois	1838	Canadians rebellious under British rule; Morse patents the telegraph; *Pickwick Papers* by Dickens is sensation in England
Breaks off engagement with Mary Todd; elected to fourth term in legislature	1840	Act of Union joins upper and lower Canada; Emerson publishes *Essays*
Recovers from year-long fits of melancholia; marries Mary Todd in Episcopal ceremony at her house in Springfield	1842	Chinese ports opened to foreign trade; Daniel Webster negotiates treaty settling Canada and America boundary dispute
Establishes law partnership with William Herndon; campaigns for Henry Clay, Whig candidate for President	1844	James Polk elected President; Dumas writes *Three Musketeers* in France
Elected as Whig to Congress	1846	Potato famine in Ireland; Melville writes first novel, *Typee*
Denounces President James Polk for Mexican War; does not run for reelection; campaigns for Zachary Taylor	1848	Louis Napoleon becomes head of France—Louis Philippe abdicates; U.S. gains California and New Mexico as result of Mexican War
Receives patent for buoyant chambers on steamboats; declines presidential appointment as governor of Oregon Territory	1849	Revolutions crushed in Italy and France; Livingstone begins exploration of Africa
Delivers eulogy of Henry Clay; campaigns for Winfield Scott, Whig candidate for President	1852	Wells Fargo (Pony Express) established; Singer manufactures first sewing machines; Harriet Beecher Stowe publishes *Uncle Tom's Cabin*

HIS LIFE	YEAR	HIS WORLD
Makes first reply to Stephen Douglas's Popular Sovereignty at Springfield; becomes Whig candidate for U.S. Senate and loses	1854	Crimean War; first Cunard steamship crossing; Henry Thoreau writes *Walden;* Whitman writes *Leaves of Grass*
Comes in second in votes for vice presidential nomination in Republican convention; supports Republican candidate John Fremont	1856	Viscount Palmerston is British prime minister; Congress of Paris ends Crimean War; Russia loses influence in Eastern Europe
Receives his largest fee for single case against Illinois Central Railroad; attacks Douglas on Dred Scott decision on fugitive slaves	1857	James Buchanan sworn in as fifteenth President; Pasteur proves fermentation is caused by living organisms
First of Lincoln-Douglas debates; wins acquittal on murder charge against Duff Armstrong	1858	Laying of Atlantic Cable; adoption of the Bessemer steel process in France
Begins to speak in all parts of the nation as potential candidate in 1860 in New York	1859	Marx writes *Das Kapital;* Henry Thoreau publishes *On Civil Disobedience;* Darwin publishes *Origin of the Species*
Delivers Cooper Union speech in New York in February; wins Republican nomination for President in Chicago in May; wins plurality and electoral majority	1860	Garibaldi leads Red Shirts to conquer Sicily and Naples; South Carolina secedes
Sworn in as President in March; Fort Sumter surrenders in April; Union Army defeated at Bull Run in July	1861	Italy united under King Victor Emmanuel

HIS LIFE	YEAR	HIS WORLD
Edwin Stanton replaces Cameron as secretary of war; U. S. Grant wins victories in Tennessee; New Orleans captured by Union Forces	1862	Bismarck becomes Chancellor (Prussia); Julia Ward Howe writes "Battle Hymn of the Republic"
Issues Emancipation Proclamation on New Year's Day; Confederates defeated at Gettysburg; Grant wins Vicksburg	1863	Maximilian proclaimed Emperor of Mexico
Nominated for second term, beats General McClellan in November; Admiral Farragut wins Battle of Mobile Bay	1864	Red Cross established; Greeks shake off Turks, write democratic constitution; Karl Marx founds the First Internationale
Inaugurated for second term; Lee surrenders at Appomattox; shot at Ford's Theater on April 14, dies next day	1865	Bismarck and Napoleon III make alliance; Tolstoy publishes *War and Peace*; *Alice in Wonderland* by Lewis Carroll published

Now he belongs to the ages.

—EDWIN STANTON
Lincoln's Secretary of War,
at Lincoln's death

Bibliography

Angle, Paul M. (ed.). *The Lincoln Reader.* New Brunswick: Rutgers University Press, 1947.

Baker, Jean. *Mary Todd Lincoln.* New York: W. W. Norton, 1987.

Basler, Roy P., Marion Dolores Pratt, and Lloyd A. Dunlap (eds.), *The Collected Works of Abraham Lincoln* (9 vols.). New Brunswick: Rutgers University Press, 1953–55.

Beveridge, Albert J. *Abraham Lincoln (1809–1858)* (2 vols.). Boston: Houghton Mifflin, 1928.

Carr, Clark E. *Lincoln at Gettysburg.* Chicago: A.C. McClurg, 1906.

Chamley, R. Z., Jr. *Lincoln's Assassins.* Boston: Little, Brown, 1937.

Charnwood, Lord [Henry]. *Abraham Lincoln.* New York: Henry Holt, 1917.

Conwell, Russell H. *Why Lincoln Laughed.* New York: Harper Bros., 1922.

Cottrell, John. *The Assassination of Abraham Lincoln.* Funk & Wagnall, 1966.

Curtis, William E. *The True Abraham Lincoln.* Philadelphia: J. B. Lippincott, 1907.

Einhorn, Louis J. *Abraham Lincoln, Orator.* Westport, CT: Greenwood Press, 1992.

Fehrenbacher, Don Edward. *Lincoln in Text and Context.* Stanford, CA: Stanford University Press, 1987.

Gross, Anthony. *Lincoln's Own Stories.* Garden City, Long Island: Garden City Press, 1912.

Hanchett, William. *The Lincoln Murder Conspiracies.* Chicago: University of Illinois Press, 1983.

Harmsberger, Caroline Thomas (ed.). *Lincoln Treasury.* Chicago: Wilcox & Follett, 1950.

Herndon, William. *Life of Lincoln.* Chicago: Albert and Charles Buni, 1930.

Hertz, Emanuel (ed.). *Lincoln Talks.* New York: Viking, 1939.

Holden, Raymond. *Lincoln, Politician and Man.* New York: Minton & Balch Co., 1929.

Kerner, Fred (ed.). *A Treasury of Lincoln Quotations.* New York: Doubleday & Co., 1965.

Kunhardt, Philip B., Jr. *A New Birth of Freedom: Lincoln at Gettysburg.* Boston: Little, Brown, 1983.

Lincoln, Rufus Rockwell (ed.). *Intimate Memories of Lincoln.* Elmira, NY: Primavera Press, 1945.

McClure, A. K. *Lincoln and Men of War-Times.* Philadelphia: Anvil Printing Co., 1892.

———. *Lincoln's Own Yarns and Stories.* Philadelphia: Anvil Printing Co., 1900.

Mearns, David (ed.). *Lincoln Papers* (2 vols.). New York: Doubleday & Co., 1948.

Mitgang, Herbert. *The Fury Trial.* New York: Viking, 1974.

Neeley, Mark, Jr. (ed.). *The Abraham Lincoln Encyclopedia.* New York: McGraw-Hill, 1982.

————. *The Last Best Hope of Earth.* Cambridge, MA: Harvard University Press, 1993.

Nevins, Allan (ed.). *Lincoln's Gettysburg Address.* Chicago: University of Illinois Press, 1954.

Nicolay, Helen. *Personal Traits of Abraham Lincoln.* New York: Century Co., 1913.

Oates, Stephen B. *With Malice Toward None.* New York: Harper & Row, 1977.

Randall, J. C. *Mr. Lincoln* (4 vols.). New York: Dodd Mead, 1945.

Sandburg, Carl. *Abraham Lincoln* (6 vols.). New York: Charles Scribner & Sons, 1943.

Selby, Paul. *Anecdotal Lincoln.* Chicago: Thompson & Thomas, 1900.

Stern, Philip Van Doren. *The Life and Writings of Abraham Lincoln.* New York: Random House, 1945.

Tarbell, Ida M. *Father Abraham.* New York: Moffat Yard & Co., 1909.

Thomas, Benjamin. *Abraham Lincoln.* New York: Alfred A. Knopf, 1952.

Turner, Justin G. and Linda Levitt Turner. *Lincoln: His Life and Letters.* New York: Alfred A. Knopf, 1972.

Villard, Henry. *Lincoln on the Eve of '61.* New York: Alfred A. Knopf, 1941.

While Lincoln Lay Dying: First Testimony Taken in Connection with the Assassination of Abraham Lincoln as Recorded by Corporal James Tanner [manuscript]. Philadelphia: Union League of Philadelphia, 1968.

Williams, T. Harry. *Lincoln and His Generals*. New York: Alfred A.
    Knopf, 1952.
Wills, Gary. *Inventing America*. New York: Doubleday & Co.,
    1978.
Wolf, William J. *The Almost Chosen People*. New York: Doubleday &
    Co., 1959.

Index